THROUGH T'MILL

**Keith Haigh
and
Jay Whittam**

MINERVA PRESS
MONTREUX LONDON WASHINGTON

THROUGH T'MILL

Copyright © Keith Haigh and Jay Whittam 1996

ISBN 1 85863 869 0

First Published 1996 by
MINERVA PRESS
195 Knightsbridge,
London SW7 1RE

Printed in Great Britain by
Antony Rowe Ltd., Chippenham, Wiltshire

THROUGH T'MILL

Foreword

It's taken almost a lifetime to write this book – Keith Haigh's life, that is. Almost two lifetimes, I suppose, if you count mine as well.

A chance remark sparked it off. I'd listened to Keith through many a winter evening recounting his stories about life and the people he has met in the mills he has worked in for so many years. Why not record these experiences for posterity? After all, the mills have all but disappeared now – or suffered a sea-change from the way they were a generation or more ago. Besides, I argued, there aren't many people still around who have gone from green apprentice to mill manager, and who have seen the good and the bad of working in textiles – for Keith, there was never an 'ugly'. Nor are there many who can recall the marvellous 'characters', and the humour, as well as the pressures of daily life in the mills.

Keith took me at my word, and his story, from his early days, is the subject of this book. There is also just a glimpse of another world, away from the mill, in which Keith and his wife, Philippa, cope with their Down's syndrome son. But that's another story.

In truth, Keith and I have had much fun putting this book together; if it informs, pleases or entertains anyone else, then that is an added pleasure for us.

Finally, our sincere thanks to those who have helped us, and encouraged us to proceed this far.

Jay Whittam

CHAPTER 1

"What do you think, then, Dad?"

"I think you could do worse, lad. I reckon it's worth giving it a go."

There was a long pause, as we sat there, facing each other, in the kitchen, my father and myself, and thought about a career in textiles.

We'd been mulling the idea over for most of the evening; it was now up to me - it was decision time, and I could feel Dad's earnest gaze fixed upon me, waiting a response.

"Right, then. I will."

My mind was made up, and for the first time in my life I was taking control of the reins. Sixteen years old, but better late than never.

Dad was pleased, I could tell, and we both knew how important that kitchen conference had been. It was the beginning of a new phase in our lives.

Eight scholarships were to be awarded locally. I'd heard about these awards from school. If you got a scholarship, that meant you could continue your education, and if you continued your education, you could get beyond the shop floor. As the saying went, you could 'get on'. Even then, I knew what I wanted - I wanted to 'get on'.

It wouldn't be easy - there was a lot of competition from youngsters like myself, keen to get 'learning a trade'. But it was the north of England, it was the 1950s, and a lad could do well for himself in textiles.

I must have put down the right things on my application form, and even made the right sort of noises at my first interview, because, before many days had passed, I found myself shortlisted for a second interview. I was just sixteen, nervous as hell, and thinking I'd wished I'd never bothered.

Looking back at myself now from the other end of my career, I can't help smiling at what I used to be like. As green as any cabbage you're ever likely to see! But eager, yes, and enthusiastic, and full of anticipation, like any teenager of that era - or were we 'adolescents' then? Or even 'juveniles'? I don't remember.

Whatever, we were full of hope, and anxious to get started on the first rung of that ladder to self-fulfilment that a good job promised us.

And how many changes I've seen over nearly half a century. For one thing; from leaving school, right through to now, I've been in employment. How much hope for a steady and permanent job is there nowadays for a great many youngsters in this country? It's a different world, and, especially, the world of the textile industry. Whatever happened to it?

I'm lying here in bed, now, in hospital, waiting for an operation in the next few days, that could make or mar the rest of my life; and yet I can picture myself, a lifetime ago, getting really worked up about meeting some men, and having nothing more fearsome to face than having to talk about myself!

It's all relative, isn't it? I mean, whether it's facing an interview when you're a youngster, or having to undergo a major heart operation when you're older, it's the same voyage into the unknown, and it's sufficient to send the same shivers down your spine. I know I'll be glad when it's all over. But we've all experienced these times in our lives, these crucial phases, and we all know how we've faced them as individuals. Perhaps, by sharing experiences, we can learn to cope better when crises loom.

Anyway, working in mills – as I have done for so many years – you meet a lot of people, and you enter a very special world. There's nothing to compare. It's like no other industry. But let's start where it all began, back at my scholarship interview.

This second interview was to take place at the local technical college. The day itself was one of those winter days when leaden clouds roll off the Pennines in the west, and cast a gloomy blanket over the towns and villages of the West Riding of Yorkshire. Walls, roads and pavements are grey and black, but the fine rain coats them with an unaccustomed sheen, and makes them glisten.

It was late in the afternoon, and dusk was already provoking a barrage of lights in homes and factories, when my dad and myself shuffled into the college.

In a sense, I suppose, it was kind of symbolic when Dad and I parted at the door. In a way, I had to show that I could cope on my own from then on. It was time for me to make my own way.

Eventually, I was shown into a room where, sitting round a large mahogany table, was a panel of 'judges'. They looked up as I entered the room, and six pairs of eyes searched mine. One or two of the seated figures nodded vaguely in my direction; a well dressed lady in a dark grey suit and white blouse smiled encouragingly; the others turned back to their papers and ignored me.

At the head of the table sat a smallish man, quite stockily built. He was smartly dressed in a grey, pinstripe suit, and a dark blue tie.

He leaned forward as I came in, and motioned me to sit down. For the next twenty minutes or so, my eyes were as if riveted on this gentleman, as he asked me questions about my home, my school, my work.

At first I blurted out answers as quickly as I could, but, as I looked at this man, his kindly eyes seemed to be willing me to say the right sort of things to please those sitting round the table. I gradually relaxed, and warmed to the promptings of these kindly eyes. Each time I answered, he nodded in agreement, as though what I'd said was the most interesting fact that anyone had ever told him. Before very long, my life story – such as it was at sixteen – was theirs in full!

Obviously, I didn't know then that that gentleman was over the next ten years going to influence the whole course of my working life, but that, indeed, was the case.

A week or so later, I received a letter informing me that I'd been successful in gaining one of the eight scholarships that had been awarded. Mam and Dad were thrilled. I, too, was pleased – naturally – but adolescent arrogance convinced me that I was right to be chosen. Humility comes with experience. Nevertheless, I often wondered what happened to the forty or so others who weren't lucky enough to get a scholarship.

For the moment, though, I could think only of my own success. I was on my way.

It goes without saying that my family were with me all the way. I was one of five children, and, if I'd been given my choice by some divine being, I couldn't have wished for a better father and mother, and brothers and sisters, and home. I was just lucky.

My father worked all his life on the railways, and we grew up close to the station in a little West Riding village, barely a stone's throw, in a manner of speaking, from the great mills that gave life to this area.

Where we lived, we were never in any doubt that we were at the heart of the woollen trade, and that that was where the parents of so many friends worked.

Growing up during the Second World War, you were too young to worry about it; you knew something big was going on, and you learned the bawdy songs about Hitler and Goebbels, and, night after night, your sleep was broken by the roar of aeroplanes flying overhead.

But what you didn't have, you didn't miss. There was school, there were friends, and there was a world to explore; the war could have been a million miles away for all we knew – or cared.

Well, that's not strictly true, on reflection; as we grew older, we came to a better understanding of what was going on.

In the early days, we never went to school without a torch, gas mask, and sandwiches; we practised fire drill every day, and we took part in endless schemes to raise money or supplies for the War Effort.

Little did I think, however, that just a few years later, I would join the textile trade, that I would see it in its heyday, at its greatest, in the 1950s, and, over the course of my working life, watch it virtually disappear.

Nor could I then have known that I would enter a world populated by some of the most interesting men and women you could ever wish to meet, marvellous, unforgettable folk, honest and hard-working people who, at the top of their trade, lived in semi-detached houses, not grand mansions, and guarded their modest wealth with care and prudence.

To become a textile man meant full-time education in college. I started my course in September, 1952, and got stuck into my work.

I'd been at college some two or three months before I met the Principal of the Textile Department, Mr James. To call him 'eccentric' would be to do him an injustice, but you could sense that he didn't inhabit quite the same world as the rest of us. His office was teeming with wool samples, books, papers, files, and nothing remotely in the place where you might reasonably expect it to be.

In the middle of this jumble he would sit and talk about the textile industry, and the pitfalls we might meet on the way. Occasionally, he would come into the lecture theatre to speak to us or to teach us textile calculations.

He would start by giving us an equation: "A warp is...," he would start, then break off to call out the attendance register. Sometimes he seemed to mumble to himself – 36, 27, 18 – and there were times when we didn't know whether he was developing the equation or finalising the numbers on the register.

As new students, we were constantly looking across to each other's scribbled notes to see whether we had included the total class number in our calculations, or added in, by mistake, the number of class hours taught. Of course, in those days, we were too much in awe of such a figure to think of asking him to repeat his instructions.

The variety of answers we submitted must have given him much cause for reflection on the academic ability of the new intake. Whereas he himself pretended that he knew nothing about the subject of textiles, we had no need to pretend – we really did know nothing. On the other hand, the books that he had written on textiles had become standard works of reference. Thus, the gulf between us was considerable, but, in time, we would learn.

That first year was an easy year – I think it was meant to be – but the following years were tough and designed to test whether we had the qualities needed to succeed.

Under the terms of our scholarship, at the end of our college year, we had to go to one of the firms which had put up the money for sponsorship. In this part of the West Riding, in the early fifties, there were textile mills on almost every street corner; it was a proverbial 'hive of industry', so there was no difficulty over finding a place to take us.

Call it luck, or fate, or whatever, but by some chance I found myself again in the office of the gentleman who had so impressed me a year earlier at my interview – the gentleman with kindly eyes. He asked me how I had got on in my first year.

I told him how much I'd enjoyed college. I really had. It had whetted my appetite for textiles. In that year, I'd studied subjects like raw materials, carding, spinning, weaving, colour design and cloth-finishing, and I felt as though I was beginning to feel my way into a new and fascinating world.

It wasn't just what you could see, and it wasn't just the purr or the rattle of the machines in the mill, and it wasn't only the feel of the wool – although that was good – but the whole atmosphere of the mill; it was things like the sharp smell of oil mixed with wool; the day-today routine; working alongside others; it created not just physical warmth, but a feeling of security, funny though that might sound to anyone outside the textile industry.

Even today, the 'sensations' to be experienced in a mill seem to make me feel elated; they seem to take away the stress and pressure of the day. Other people go for walks, play cricket or bowls or golf, or kick a ball, go swimming – or a hundred and one other 'relaxing' pursuits. For me, I get just as much relaxation by walking through a mill. That's how much I came to love the environment of the mill, and how much it soon became a part of my life.

"Well, lad," he asked at length, "would you like to come and work for us?"

At that time, I wasn't sure who I wanted to work for.

"Look," he said, "if you want to come and work for us, and you're prepared to get your hands mucky, we'll show you what it's all about."

Blunt speech, kindly eyes, and the promise of a thorough grounding were quite sufficient to convince me.

And so I started work with what, for me, was the best firm in the valley – Joseph Newton's, established long before the turn of the century.

I wasn't the only one who thought so – the firm had customers enough to bear out that boast. It was a firm that was prepared to innovate schemes, prepared to go to any lengths to produce the finest materials, prepared to back schemes of apprenticeship to catch the best apprentices – a firm, in fact, you were proud to work for.

They were everything you'd expect of the premier woollen manufacturers in the town. The mill buzzed with energy from dawn to dusk, creating wealth for the town and its population, making wonderful cloths, mainly for the ladies' trade.

The mill itself nestled at the foot of a very steep hill, approached from the rear down a twisting road flanked on either side by neat terrace houses blackened by years of smoke that had billowed from hearth and factory chimney. A railway ran across the back of the mill, and the approach from the rear was through a quaintly arched, Victorian railway bridge.

Between the mill and the railway line was a coal-blackened track known as the 'coil rally', or coal road, down which the coal used to be transported from the station to all the mills which stood in lines along the main road from Bentley to Dewsfield.

The front of the mill, by contrast, standing alongside the main road, was neat and tidy, with large wooden gates, and an office entrance to the red-brick mill, always with the brass gleaming and smart.

It was here that I saw for myself, for the first time, the various processes of cloth manufacture – the wool sorting, willeying, carding and spinning – and on through to the weaving and finishing departments; and then there were the pungent smells of each place, sharp and distinct; as you moved from department to department you knew exactly where you were, recognising each different process by its unique smell.

It was then, without a doubt that I 'got the bug', that is, I knew that this was where I wanted to spend my working life. To see the finished product, the beautiful cloth, and to know how and by what processes it had arrived at that stage was, for me, an exciting and new experience. I knew I'd chosen the right career.

The firm's managing director was a great figure of a man. There was no doubting who was in charge. His office was the 'ivory tower'; nobody like us ever approached that place.

Occasionally, he would descend from his tower, and, coming among us, would strut around, paternally questioning if all were well. If we were not doing the job right, his paternal air would slip, and he would tell us in no uncertain terms where we were going wrong.

We learned fast, time slipped by, and, even before we knew it, our apprenticeship came rapidly to a close. It was good to be a young man in a man's world; you no longer felt you were a young lad; this wasn't school; you were learning because that was what you wanted to do. And you were paid for it – not much, admittedly, but at least you were paid.

On the last day of an apprenticeship at the mill, each apprentice would be summoned to the big office, the 'ivory tower', to appear before the M.D. With its oak beams, and its oak panelling, and dark leather chairs, there was something faintly Dickensian about the place, yet sufficiently grand to inspire a feeling of awe and wonder. It almost seemed as though Mr Jaggers would suddenly enter the room, cursing roundly.

My turn came in due course; this would be about the mid-1950s, as near as I can guess. The foreman stopped me as I was about to enter.

"When you get in there, lad, he'll say to you: 'Now that you've finished your apprenticeship, I suppose you'll know all there is to know about this place.' He always says that."

And then the foreman said: "You've got to stand there, and say that you'll never stop learning. Do you hear what I say? You'll never stop learning. And that'll make his day. You understand? Now don't forget to say that."

Shortly after, I was summoned into this great office, and there was the great T.J., Mr Timothy Johnson, the managing director, sitting on a high-backed chair at that enormous table. He peered at me as I entered, fixing me over the top of his half-moon glasses.

"What's your name, then, young man?"

I told him my name.

"Today you finish your apprenticeship, is that right?"

"Yes, sir."

"And today you'll be allocated to a department. I suppose, now, you'll know all there is to know about this place, then, is that it?"

"Sir," I said, "I'll never stop learning."

He peered at me closely, and he smiled.

"What a lovely answer! I'm right pleased to hear you say that."

He must have said the same thing to every apprentice that went through his office, but, in those days, tradition was important, and, if tradition was to be upheld, then apprentices were not the ones to rock the boat. No apprentice would ever stop learning. At least he was pleased – or appeared to be – and that pleased us minnows.

Since those days, so much has changed; I doubt whether many today would worry a great deal about it. But we did, then.

From then on, my career in textiles started in earnest.

I was allocated to the Blending Department. The Blending Office was a small, dark, dingy room in those days. At one end sat the colour matcher; he was a curious little man with a rather odd but gentle sense of humour. It was the colour matcher's job, as you might expect, to match the colours of the different wools so that, when they were sent to the Spinning Department, they were correct. Any mistake at this stage would be his fault, and mistakes could cost the firm a great deal of money.

He was surrounded by hundreds of different coloured wool samples. He would mix and blend, and then send these blended wools to the Sample Carding Room, where they'd be put together by a sample carder. He'd then bring them back into the office for us to make a pad.

Now, as a trainee colour matcher, my job was to do the 'padding up'. My desk was right at the other end of the office, which, I suppose, put me in my place. Two or three times a day, coloured wool samples would come in, and I would have to make these horrible pads, wash them and soak them till I got them nicely felted up, and then I'd have to take them over, across to the other end of this long office, for inspection and approval by the colour matcher.

I remember the colour matcher well; his name was Fred Braithwaite, and he served the firm for many years. Nothing flustered him; he carried on his job from day to day, and there was nothing he liked doing more. He was also a good man to work with.

Though I didn't particularly care for the job of padding up, he spent a lot of time showing me how to get the different effects and how to mix the different colours.

There was something about him, something in his manner, in the way he spoke, in the way he introduced me to the art of blending, that made me keen to work with him. I couldn't have had a better tutor to show me the industry in its most absorbing and fascinating light, and from the very beginning we got on well together. I owe him a great deal, even though it is now many years since we parted company. The last I heard of him he was a grand old man, still living in his little semi at the top of the hill overlooking the mill, where he'd lived all his working life. He deserved a long and happy retirement.

In this Blending Office, there was a metal trough, and a bar of soap next to it. I used to have to rub the pads on this soap to get them correct. Of course, the soap would wear out fairly quickly, and I had to go to the Cloth-finishing Department where it was kept.

The cloth-finishing foreman was a huge, burly individual who used to frighten the living daylights out of me. He'd go into the Cloth-milling Department, and stand there in front of the milling machine, measuring the cloth, and continuing to measure it until it was down to the correct width.

In the corner of the room he used to have a cupboard which was full to the top with soap, and he looked after those bars of soap as if they were ingots of gold. To get a bar of soap out of him was like taking a bone from a ravenous hound. And he used to glower at me every time I walked in. A snake could not have fixed me more intently.

"What's tha want, lad?"

He'd stop what he was doing, and just stare.

"Excuse me, er ... er ... Mr Jackson. Can I have another bar of soap, please?"

There was an uncomfortable silence, as the foreman glared at me. Oliver Twist knew the feeling well!

"Why, bloody 'ell, lad," he'd snarl. "You'd a bar o'soap last bloody week. What's tha doin' wi' it? Eatin' it?"

Always belligerent, always aggressive, as though not to give out a bar of soap was a matter of personal pride. In my early days, I used to be terrified of him, to the point where I used to sneak into the room; if he wasn't there, I'd go to the cupboard to see if the lock was off – he used to keep it padlocked most of the time. But if he happened to have left the lock undone for any reason, I would pinch a bar of soap and speed back to the Blending Office to do my pads, glad and relieved that I didn't have to face him again for another few days.

What a fearsome character he was! I can see his scowling face even now – it was the stuff of which nightmares are made.

Arthur Stockton was another chap who comes vividly to mind from this period in my life. Arthur was the works engineer, and he it was who governed the lives of all the mill's employees. He was the one responsible for the operation and maintenance of the steam engine.

This steam engine supplied power to all the machines in the mill; the whole factory ran from a single steam engine. This engine was linked to a line shaft, and from this line shaft every loom and every machine worked. If the steam engine broke down, then the whole mill would come to a sudden halt – it was as simple as that.

Obviously the Engine Room was a key place in the mill; from memory, I think it used to be called 'The Citadel', and inside the building was this massive, marvellous, powerful Victorian monster of an engine. It had an enormous fly-wheel, huge and spinning as smooth as silk, breathing superhuman power. Arthur used to boast that, if he stood a threepenny bit on the frame by this fly-wheel, there would be so little vibration that the threepenny bit would not fall over. I could believe it.

Though Arthur himself used to walk around in dirty overalls and a dirty flat cap, he looked after the inside of his Engine Room as if it were Buckingham Palace. You weren't allowed inside with your shoes on; you'd to take off your shoes, no matter who you were, or how important you thought you were; and it didn't matter what sort of weather it was, your shoes had to come off. You'd walk in there, and the linoleum floor was spotlessly clean. Everything was shining brass, and there was the heady smell of oil and steam in the air – and it was a very special place.

As for Arthur himself, he was a bit of a know-all. Whatever the topic, he thought he had the answer, and he liked to let people know his views; he'd boast to us apprentices that anything we wanted to know he could tell us about. In many ways he was a typical bore, with an over-inflated idea of his own ability, and we didn't particularly care for his patronising treatment.

For us apprentices, though, he got cut down to size on one of the mill outings. The coach had stopped at a roadside café – this was in the days when the mill would close down for the day, and all the employees would join the excursion to the seaside, to Filey, or Bridlington, or Scarborough or Blackpool. You didn't miss these trips, not if you could help it.

On this occasion, we all trooped into one of the roadside cafés on the way, to refresh ourselves, as usual.

Taking the lead, Arthur, knowing all there is to know about anything and nothing, ordered first. He ordered coffee.

"Will you have black or white, sir?" said the young waitress, politely.

"I'll have black, lass."

We ordered, and soon she returned with our orders. Just as she was turning away, Arthur called out, "Eh, lass; where's t'bloody milk, then?"

And that really was a revelation for us – that Arthur, who knew all there was to know, didn't know that black coffee was coffee without milk. This fount of all wisdom for us apprentices was, from that day on, a dry source; we never again took him seriously, and he knew it.

Just in case anyone has an axe to grind, I know there are people these days who say you shouldn't call coffee 'black' or 'white', because it's something to do with race. To me, that's a lot of mischief. I've never met any of our workers – except one, perhaps, and I'll tell you about her later – who complained about black or white coffee.

One final thought about Arthur. It's odd how an incident as trivial and as inconsequential as this should stay so clearly in the memory, when thousands of matters of greater import have slipped into oblivion. Kingdoms have waxed and waned since then, and been forgotten, but Arthur's blunder lives on – for me, anyway. Clay-footed gods is a phrase that comes to mind.

I suppose such a thing shouldn't matter, really; after all, there are thousands of know-alls who are not half so good at their job as Arthur was at his, and even fewer who could boast of balancing on edge a threepenny bit on an engine that ran so smoothly that the coin would not fall over.

There were plenty of young men working at the mill, some, apprentices like myself, others, doing the menial tasks of sweeping and clearing, learning the hard way about the textile trade.

With so many women also employed, the mill provided opportunity for much social intercourse, and plenty of good-natured banter between the sexes. I soon learned that most of the women could more than hold their own, when it came to the daily free-for-all on the shop floor – verbally speaking – and some of these women operatives were capable of endowing a situation with language sufficient to make your hair curl.

I learned early not to arouse the antagonism of these women. Brought up in the harsh, post-war conditions in the heart of industrial Yorkshire, many of these women had packed a lot of living into their short lives, and survival had bred a remarkable toughness and resilience in them. Their normal conversation was loud, and meant to carry beyond the incessant rattle and clatter of the machines. Their laughter was shrill and piercing, sometimes raucous and harsh, but they were women who were determined to rise above the miserable, depressing monotony of millwork, and seek the lighter side of life.

These women would often put up with a great deal from some of the men, provided that the men didn't interfere with the women's work. Woe betide any man who came between them and their quite lucrative piecework by stopping them from working. Earning their money was their prime concern, and they didn't like anything or anyone interfering with that purpose in their lives.

There was one particular young man there – I tell the story as it was told to me, happening, as it did, before I joined the firm – who thought that all women were there for his amusement.

Stan was probably about seventeen or eighteen, tall and well built, and quite handsome, in the mode of the day. He cut quite a figure for the women of the mill – and he knew it. He knew how to make them laugh, and that made him very popular – for a time.

Scarcely a day went by without Stan seeking the attention of one or other of the young women on the shop floor, and I've no doubt he had his successes – if the general bawdy talk we used to overhear was anything to go by. He was quite a lad.

Unfortunately, he 'couldn't carry corn', as the saying goes, and his success with the ladies went to his head. His banter, in time, grew thin, and his cocksure attitude began to grate.

Eventually, the women got fed up with him. He became a thorough nuisance, and it didn't go down well when the women were prevented from getting on with their work. He also became rather too 'handy' for the likes of some of the women, who reckoned he was getting above himself, especially those who felt he had taken advantage of them.

It must have been the last week before the Christmas break one year, as I understand, that he got his 'come-uppance', and the women decided that enough was enough.

Stan had been 'chasing' one particular girl for some time. Susan was probably two or three years younger than he was, not long out of school, fresh-faced, pretty, and innocent as the day is long. She was a lovely girl, and she didn't like Stan's over-familiarity.

Of course, as these things often turn out, the more she dismissed him and sought to ignore him, the greater grew the challenge, in his own mind, to bring her into his little harem. He was not used to being rejected.

The situation came to a head one afternoon when something that he either said or did to this young girl reduced her to tears. I think he'd 'tried it on' once too often, by all accounts.

When the other women around her tried to remonstrate with Stan, he told them in straight terms where to go and to mind their own business.

That was the last straw. By dint of a simple trick, they managed to corner him in one of the stock rooms. There must have been nine or ten of the women involved. They were led by a woman whom the other workers knew as 'Big Barbara' – the mind boggles! A formidable lady, I understand, by any stretch of the imagination, and the sort who would rip up telephone books for relaxation.

What happened next does not bear repeating, but their solution to the problem was prolonged and painful for this young man; he limped out of that stock room a good quarter of an hour later, very much chastened by their treatment of him.

He never again caused offence to the women on the shop floor, and, apparently, he left the firm soon after.

Rough justice, and swift punishment. It was not only his credibility that suffered that day in the stock room.

When I came to the mill, the story was still fresh in the minds of many of the workers, and I suppose what the women did to deflate that young man's ego grew with each telling of the story. Suffice to say, the substance of what I heard appears to be true; only the lurid details varied! You'd only to mention Stan by name, and there would be some very knowing nods and laughs from some of the women on the shop floor. Big Barbara and her friends ruled the roost.

All this was new to me, especially this closing ranks. The women saw to it, despite occasional individual flare-ups – mainly over boyfriends – that they helped each other when there was trouble. They provided a source of strength, as well as a shoulder to cry on. These girls who came straight into the mill from school seemed to be either very worldly wise, or desperately innocent, and, sadly, it was, more often than not, the 'nice' kids from the 'nice' homes who used to get into trouble.

At fifteen, these innocent ones, probably through ignorance, possibly flattered by the close attentions of older men, were the ones most likely to become pregnant.

On more than one occasion, the girl would leave to have her baby, and return to work as soon as possible, leaving the child to be brought up through the day with grandmother, as if it were a younger brother or sister.

There would be, obviously, a certain amount of gossip, and some tut-tutting from some in the community, but it was all kept fairly quiet, and the women in the mill would see to it that the girl got as much help and advice as they were able to offer.

There certainly seemed more tolerance than condemnation, and the attitude adopted by the women appeared to anticipate the, supposedly, more enlightened attitudes of more recent years.

Having said that, I think this charity stopped short on at least one occasion I heard of, when one of the local mill owners got a girl into trouble, and, later, married her. To compound the issue, the girl committed thereafter the worst crime of all – in their eyes – of putting on 'airs and graces'. Absolutely unforgivable.

It was only in after years, with increasing maturity and experience, that I began to appreciate the strength, unity and determination of this shop floor sisterhood.

About that time, as I recall, the firm gave me a sort of corner office next to Fred Braithwaite's, the colour matcher. It came out of the blue that I should now move into this office, which I was to share with two of the wool clerks – "so I could be on hand if Fred needed anything", I was told.

These wool clerks used to be perched up on high stools, working with enormous ledgers propped up on the sloping tops of their desks. They were important people in the mill, and for me to be working alongside them was obviously promotion; I felt that I was making progress, and that I was going up the line.

I'd not been moved in very long when, one day, the phone rang;

"Look sharp, lad!" said Fred, with some degree of urgency in his voice. "T.J.'s on his way down. He's paying us a visit."

If he'd announced that the king and queen had been coming, he couldn't have caused greater consternation than he did with his announcement that T.J. was coming to the Blending Office. This was certainly a big occasion, and we knew it.

A few minutes later, the door opened, and in walked the M.D., the great T.J.

"Good morning."

"Good morning, sir."

It was like being back at school. The directors were very remote figures, very aloof, and light years away from the run-of-the-mill people like us. You only spoke to them if they spoke to you – not like the way things are today. Perhaps that's one of the good things about today – bosses are human beings.

"I've just come to see what you're all doing. Who are you, young man?"

"Keith Haigh, sir," I replied.

"Keith ... ?"

"Haigh, sir"

He surveyed the pads I'd just completed.

"You're learning this job, I suppose, Keith?"

"Yes, sir."

He seemed to be taking an extraordinary interest in me.

"And how long have you been working in this department, then?"

"Well, about a year, I think, sir."

"And are you any good at this colour matching?"

"Yes, I think so. I seem to be picking it up quite well."

There was a pause, as he picked up one of the pads I'd made up.

"I've just read an article," he went on, "in a fashion magazine, which was saying that the new shade for this year is going to be 'pheasant'. What do you think about that?"

"Er... I'm not sure. Er... very interesting," I mumbled, unsure what the correct reply should be.

"Right, Keith, I'll be coming down to this office again next week," he said, "and I shall want you to make me a shade that you think will be called 'pheasant', and maybe we'll make some cloth called 'pheasant'. There you are, lad. Get on with it."

And with that, he strolled out of the office, leaving me absolutely flabbergasted.

The thought of trying to blend wool to match the colour of a pheasant filled me with horror.

I went over to Fred.

"Heard him, lad. It's nowt to do wi' me. He's asked you to do it, so you'd better get on wi' it."

"But what am I going to do, Fred?"

I think he could hear the touch of panic in my voice.

He said, "Well, if it were up to me, I'd get on mi bike and get up to the park. There's a museum in the park, and in the museum they've got pheasants in glass cages, plenty o' t' beggars. Go and tek a good look at one."

"Oh, crikey!" I thought.

But I got on my bike, and rode up the steep hill, through the avenue of trees to the beautiful Victorian mansion that once was the proud home of a notable gentleman and local benefactor, and now the local museum.

I soon found a glass case with a stuffed pheasant in it, and just stared at the array of colours in its plumage.

Now, if you've ever looked really closely at a pheasant, you'll know what I mean. The colours are beautiful – fawn, chocolate brown, cream and white, orange, and many different shades in between. Such a blend is a feast to the eyes, and a glorious example of nature's willingness to combine camouflage with beauty. But all I could see then were the problems – and no easy solution.

"How the heck am I going to make a blend of wool looking like a blummin' pheasant?" I chuntered to myself. "It's impossible."

I left the museum, and free-wheeled back down to the mill, lost in thought.

"It can't be done," I told Fred, when I got back. "I wouldn't know where to start."

I didn't get a lot of sympathy from him on this occasion.

"Well, you'd better get to know, and pretty quick, because, if you 'aven't done it for next week... use your initiative, lad," he said, poking a bony finger at me.

I thought for a while. I thought, "Well, the best thing I can do is to go and get a pheasant."

So, I borrowed money from my dad and went into town to the market, and there I bought a pheasant. I took it back to the mill and put it in a big drawer that I had under my desk.

For the next few days, I struggled. I kept opening the drawer and matching up my bits of wool, and putting them together on bits of this pheasant.

Mills, of course, are quite warm places, and after three or four days people would come into the office, wrinkle their nose, give Fred and I a very worried look, then, without a word, beat a hurried retreat. The two wool clerks, perched high on their office stools barely a few yards away, were in a state of insurrection. Only bribery prevented outright mutiny.

A week quickly passed. True to his word, the managing director returned. By this time, of course, the pheasant was being very anti-social.

"Now, then, er... Keith, is it?" he said. "How are you getting on with your pheasant?"

"Very well, Mr Johnson," I replied, confidently. "I've made one or two pads here."

I showed him what I'd done.

"Do you think that that looks like a pheasant?" he asked, looking down at me with a rather strange glint in his eye.

"Well, er, I think it is, Mr Johnson," I said. He examined it more closely.

"That's a pretty good effort, lad, I think. Oh, by the way, have a bath some time – you're not smelling too fresh."

And with that, he departed. I didn't mention the pheasant to him, but a number of people were glad to see it go. I can't remember whether the firm made any pheasant-coloured cloth or not, but it provided a good learning experience – and a good laugh in the mill for those who knew what I'd done.

About the same time, Reg Robinson was in charge of wool-buying. This was the same gentleman whom I had first met at my interview the man with the kindly eyes. (How strange to recall such a detail so many years on from then.)

For quite some time we worked together, and, as I grew more experienced, I was drawn more into the discussions about the wool we would buy – the blending and the wool-buying departments had to work closely together.

Each morning we would go through what was to be bought, and Reg and I worked with a special kind of rapport between us. Over the years I got to know him well, and if there were any problems I always used to go and speak with him; he was a great help and adviser, and I learned a lot about wool and the industry from him.

After I'd been at Newton's for some eight years – this must be about 1960 – I decided that the time had come for me to think about spreading my wings. I looked at Fred; he'd been in this mill all his working life. He knew his job, but his field was limited. In truth, the time seemed right for me to sample other things outside this mill. There were worlds other than wool blending to conquer.

For a young, apprentice-trained lad like myself, opportunities and openings in those days were plentiful. I'd been very happy for those years at Newton's, but now it was time to move on, and the place to move on to, the place in vogue, was the shoddy trade. In the late fifties and early sixties, shoddy was a very prosperous industry, mainly centred on the town of Oversett, in the heart of the West Riding. However, a vacancy arose not far from where I was living, and so I applied.

It was a firm that specialised in shoddy manufacture – 'shoddy' you understand, in the true sense of the word, that is, cloth made from shredded rags.

I got the job. I remember well the day I had to tell old Reg that I'd got the job and was leaving the mill. He was extremely upset. He talked to me; he even rang my father, asking him to try to persuade me to change my mind. But I was young and my mind was made up. Eventually, Reg came to see me.

"Well, lad, I wish you all the best. I'll obviously give you a good reference..." He was too upset to say much more. To this day, I still have that reference, and the memory of a good, honest, hardworking gentleman, with kindly eyes.

Thus, in 1960, I started out on a new job, a new venture which was a completely different kettle of fish. This was the mungo trade – a trade always looked upon as the cheap end of the market. The industry provided cheap material to act as fillers to go in with the wool to make the various blends for the mills up and down the district.

The mill itself was situated on the outskirts of the town, straddling both sides of a quiet road. Age and pollution had seen to it that the stonework was shiny black.

On one side of the road stood the mill itself. There was a small office, and, to it was connected a row of terrace houses owned by the company and used to house workers over the years. Behind the office and houses stood the low, small sheds of the rag-pulling and dyehouse. A pall of steam and smoke hung permanently in the air in and around these sheds, as the work went on. But worse still; at the rear of these sheds was the dreaded carbonising mill, with trucks of rags constantly driven in and out on small tracks.

On the other side of the road stood the warehouse and despatch department, which was always extremely busy, with lorries coming and going with their loads of material.

As mills go, it was obviously quite small, but that didn't prevent it from becoming a most prosperous mill.

Fratton & Sons was run by a former RAF Officer – and what a character he turned out to be! He lived some fifty miles from the mill at a little village up in the Yorkshire Dales. He had an office in the mill, and every morning he'd set off from home about six o'clock for work. He'd arrive at the mill, but, before he started any work, one of the employees was detailed to prepare two eggs and two rashers of bacon for him for his breakfast. No matter what emergency might arise, it had to wait until he'd finished his breakfast.

Each year, we were expected to go up to Brunsedge in the Dales, near to where he lived, and near where the Fell Races take place. He didn't send us up the fell, but he did expect us, all the employees, to take part in the festivities, and we enjoyed every minute of our stay there. It was good fun.

Amongst other things, we helped to organise the annual Fell Race, which was an important date in the village calendar. We got to know the runners, and marvelled at their stamina in being able to complete such a course. Our own stamina was tested to the full, later in the day, by retiring to Wing Commander Fratton's house to consume his ample stock of liquor!

That was the thing in those days; it wasn't just a job – it was far more than that. You had to take part, and what the bosses said, you didn't question.

If the fun of the days out was one thing, the dyehouse at the mill was completely different. You can't imagine a bigger contrast between the fresh air and the open fields and woods of Brunsedge, to which we went each summer, and the evil-smelling, dingy and cramped conditions of the dyehouse.

What a place that was! You'd have to see it to believe it could exist in the twentieth century – but it did!

The raw rags used to come in to be dyed. They were sorted into different qualities, put into large vats open to the elements, and boiled.

You'd go there on a winter evening, and the place would be full of steam, and through the steam you'd see the indistinct shapes of men poling the rags; the men used to move round huge vats and turn the rags, using long poles – what an awful job that was! And the stench was indescribable.

The men would boil up the rags until they got the colour just right.

The rags were then dried off in a big dryer, and then taken down to the blending room where they were all layered out and blended, and put through rag machines which brought them back into fibrous form. That, briefly, was the shoddy, or mungo, trade.

It was a terrible place to spend your working life, but the job had to be done by someone – the men who did that job had drawn the occupational short straw, and I was glad that I wasn't one of them.

But if the dyehouse was bad, the carbonising room was infinitely worse. It was an appalling place, almost nightmarish.

Workmen used to take the rags, put them into trucks, wheel them into another building, and then pump hydrochloric acid gas into the building where the rags were placed in sealed compartments, and the gas used to dissolve all the cottons in the material.

One of the reasons why the shoddy trade progressed so well in the fifties and sixties was that the only foreign fibre that was used, other than wool, was cotton, and cotton was easy to deal with – the cotton was dissolved out of the rags at an early stage.

On one occasion, I went in there, not understanding the processes of the operation, having just the day before bought myself what I considered to be a very smart pair of cotton warp trousers.

What I hadn't realised – but very soon did – was that, as I was working in and out of the carbonising room through the day, my trousers would begin to disintegrate, and, by the end of the day, these very same smart trousers of a few hours earlier were in pieces – and I was in danger of indecent exposure.

I thus learned quickly the need to avoid working in anything containing cotton when I was in and around the carbonising room. But, oh dear, it was a terrible place. Today's Health and Safety Inspectors would have had a field day.

I also began to learn that work is not just about knowing how to do a job, but about how to understand people. Miss Emily, for example.

Miss Emily was a force to be reckoned with. She lived in one of the terrace houses adjoining the mill, so that she was never far from her work.

She was, as I recall her now, an elderly, spinster-like lady, if I may use that expression, who was responsible for keeping the accounts; she was the cashier, and a most formidable lady.

People crossed her at their peril, and those who had tried to soon found out how sharp her tongue could be – sharp enough to bring grown men near to tears, if she put her mind to it.

Her weekly routine would have raised a few eyebrows, were it followed today. Every Friday, week in, week out, she would catch the bus into Dewsfield; she used to go straight to the bank to pick up the wages for all the employees, and then she would go and do her shopping! Often the wages would be secure in a string bag. She would come back to the bus station, catch the bus back to the mill, and bring the considerable sum of wages with her.

And that was the routine she'd followed for nearly thirty years, without any problems or difficulties. Even more surprising was that all the employees and local people knew her routine, and nobody used to take any special notice of it – and she herself regarded it of little consequence.

I hesitate to think what might be the likely outcome of following that routine in today's world, sadly; but innocence, and belief in the innate goodness of humanity, protected Miss Emily all her days. Perhaps, too, she might have talked any would-be assailants into submission, if ever the need had arisen.

As for our M.D., the distinguished Wing Commander Fratton, it is unfair to recall how partial he was to a tipple, whenever the occasion arose. He should be better remembered for other, good qualities. Nevertheless, memory can be oddly selective.

It was quite normal for him to live his daily routine somewhat the worse for wear and slightly 'under the weather'. But he was pleasant with it – not like some who become aggressive or irritable when affected by drink. If you kept your distance, you could hardly tell; if you were close to him, you knew pretty well! In his customary state, he was a most amiable gentleman.

He used to have four mills in his group, and at Christmas he felt obliged to visit each one in turn. Naturally, he would also feel duty-bound to share in the festivities and sample their hospitality at their Christmas fuddle, or party.

One particular year, he'd paid his customary visit to the other branches, finally arriving at our mill. One look at the state he was in told us all about the hospitality he'd obviously already enjoyed. Even before he joined in with our celebrations, he was, not to put too fine a point on it, blotto.

Somewhat reluctantly, we lifted him out of his car – it was a brand new E-type Jaguar, the first I'd seen. He stayed – heaven knows how – for the best part of two hours, and in that time continued to drink quite steadily. He tried hard to play the part of the genial guest; his hands tremblingly clutched his glass, his mouth was set in a fixed apology of a grin, but his legs had already gone home.

By the time he was ready to leave, I don't think he knew whether it was Good Friday or Easter Sunday. (Actually, it was Christmas Eve!)

Somehow, responding to his mumbled request, three of us got him back into his car and squeezed him into the driver's seat – no mean feat when you consider that none of his bones or muscles seemed to be connected to any other parts of his anatomy. He sat there for a few moments – we were very reluctant for him even to contemplate driving in his condition, but he insisted – with a faraway look in his eyes.

Then, with a supreme effort of concentration, he fumbled blindly, until the ignition key blundered into the lock. The engine roared into life, and, with a cheery wave and a muffled shout, he sped off into the night.

We stood for a while, in silence, listening for what should have been the inevitable crunch of metal, but nothing came to us, save the roar of a very powerful engine diminishing in the cold night air, and, closer at hand, the raucous music of the party inside, blaring out that it was Christmas.

How he ever got back to the Dales that night, I shall never know. Perhaps it is possible, after all, to have more than one miracle at Christmas!

CHAPTER 2

With the festivities confined once again to the stuff of memory for another year, we all returned quickly to the realities of getting and spending, and working hard to do so.

To belong to a Textile Society was essential. If you really intended to make progress up the management ladder, it was absolutely necessary to join your local Society.

Every local town had its own Society – the Dewsfield Textile Society, the Morthorpe Textile Society, the Bentley Textile Society etc. I had chosen to be in the Dewsfield Society.

Meetings of the Society were held in smoky little rooms after work, and it was at these meetings that people would explain new ideas and new techniques, or the latest machinery.

This was really where we learned about the state of the industry, and it was marvellous to be able to mix with these men who knew the textile trade from top to bottom; their accumulated wealth of expertise and experience in textiles gave them a solidity and permanence, a platform of stability that would be rare to find today. To speak with them on a regular basis was an education in itself.

At one of the meetings, we had a speaker from a firm in Potterton talking to us about a mill over in Ireland, and, as it happened, the firm was looking for an assistant manager.

It seemed to me to be an opportunity too good to be missed. I'd had enough of the shoddy trade by this time – it had been good for me and I'd learned a great deal, but I didn't feel that I wanted to carry on working in that particular sphere much more. Here was an opportunity for me to take a first step on the managerial ladder. Besides, relations with my immediate boss – a chap called John Sykes – had deteriorated, and we simply didn't see eye to eye on a number of issues.

I asked Joe Thompson, the speaker, if he'd interview me for this post of Assistant Manager.

"Yes," he said, "but you'll have to come with me to Ireland."

Some days later I received a phone call. It was Joe.

"I'm going to Ireland on Saturday morning. If you want this job, lad, you'll have to come out and see the managing director."

The year was 1962. That Saturday morning, Joe and I flew out from what used to be Yeadon Airport, and travelled to the wilds of Ireland – and that flight was quite an experience! We were buffeted all over the place by winds that tossed the small plane about in the air, like a child's toy, and left us with stomachs where, formerly, our mouths used to be. It was not pleasant. It was a bumpy ride all the way – but not half so bumpy as the life I would be leading in the next few months.

We arrived late on Saturday evening – glad, speaking personally, to have arrived at all! – at a little town on the west coast of Ireland. It's a place I have visited quite regularly since, but, to me, then, it seemed as remote as Siberia – a very desolate place indeed, and I wondered even then whether I'd made a mistake in going there. My wife, Philippa, was expecting our first child, in England, and I was a long way away in an emergency.

In complete contrast with the mill I'd just left, the mill I had now come to was modern – at least, modern in the terms of the day. It was set on the edge of the town, which could best be described as resembling a wild west town with nothing at either end, except a road leading to nowhere in particular.

Towards the middle was a solitary public house, and near the public house was a railway station where trains, on a good day, called twice. I hardly think that the Station Master, who lived in a small, neat cottage next to the station, would have died of overwork.

There was one hotel nearby, and that was the 'Railway Hotel'! What else could it have been! That was to be 'home' for a while.

When, eventually, the job was offered, I took it. We all make mistakes in our lives, but this was to be one of the biggest in my life.

Even then, leaving Fratton's was deliberately made difficult and unpleasant for me by John Sykes. I had the feeling he had tried to stick his oar in to prevent my getting the job in Ireland.

The new position was fine. I liked the place, I liked the people I was working with day by day, and there was opportunity to learn. It was not that.

The problem was the managing director, Frank Dover. He was an autocrat – and unpleasant with it – and not in the same mould as people in the textile trade that I'd known hitherto, with, possibly, the exception of John Sykes.

I knew almost from the first week that I was never going to get on with him. To look at, he was a thin-faced, seedy-looking man, devoid of all charisma. He'd been chief clerk at a mill in Bradford, before he'd been offered this M.D.'s job in Ireland. In today's world, he'd never have survived – he simply wasn't good enough. His major problem, I suppose, came down to man-management; he'd no idea how to communicate, no easy manner with his employees; no way of inspiring confidence, or trust, or respect. In fact, he had very little to offer at all.

His sole interests were his work and his religion. He was a devout Anglican, and he and his wife attended church regularly. I can't think of a worse advertisement for Christian charity. Even during my first week in Ireland, I became very aware of this fact. He rang me up on the Saturday night.

"Keith," he said, "do you go to church, or chapel, or what?"

His manner was always brusque, and devoid of common courtesy.

"Well," I said, eager to impress, "I usually go to church. I was a choirboy for some years."

Why I should think that that titbit of information would impress him, I don't know.

"Good," he replied. "I'll pick you up at half past nine tomorrow morning. You can come to church with us."

Just like that. It dawned on me soon after that there might be a problem.

I thought, "My God! Is he a Roman Catholic? I forgot to make it clear I'm Church of England." Potentially, this could prove an embarrassing encounter.

The following morning, at nine thirty, he was outside the door, ready and waiting. I felt a bit apprehensive, and, not wishing to make a fool of myself, decided against asking him to which denomination he belonged. Wait and hope that all would be well.

We set off, and, after a lengthy drive along quiet lanes that opened up breathtaking vistas of beautiful green countryside – here was spiritual inspiration of itself - we eventually arrived at a small church that nestled unobtrusively on the edge of a village. By this time, we were so far away from anything that resembled civilisation, I was amazed to find that people actually lived here.

Recollections of the song about a 'chapel in the valley' came to mind, but this chapel was not even in the valley; it was way out in the sticks, somewhere on the more remote reaches of the west coast of Ireland. But, though so isolated and wild, there was a rugged beauty and a freshness about the place that could not fail to impress. It felt good, somehow, to be there that Sunday morning.

Inside, the church was very plain – white walls and darkwood pews, pleasant and homely. The service was unremarkable, as was the vicar who intoned the prayers with a soft, lilting voice. He announced the hymn – 'Onward Christian Soldiers' – and from the chancel the harmonium struck up the opening chords.

I turned to look at the source of this resounding tune that bounced the sound from wall to whitewashed wall of the little chapel. It stirred the heart to hear it.

My wandering gaze fell upon, first, the organ stool, and, secondly, perched very solidly on it, the considerable rump of the middle-aged lady who was pumping the harmonium so vigorously as she played.

I was fascinated. Her bulk swayed to and fro, and, as it did so, her enormous posterior overlapped each side of the stool in turn, rhythmically squashed and stretched, squashed and stretched as she swayed, marching 'as to war', like some huge bellows that served to provide power for the harmonium. It was an unforgettable sight, and I had to turn away my gaze, consciously breaking the spell of this hypnotic, heaving, woolskirted flesh.

There was Frank Dover, unsmiling and taut with fervent concentration; next, his wife, suitably serious, singing with much gusto in a rather reedy voice; one other middle-aged lady member of the congregation; and myself. We sang heartily 'Onward Christian Soldiers', but I felt completely out of place; the whole scene was so unreal and faintly ridiculous. I could hardly stop myself from furtively glancing across every now and then to watch this swaying mass of flesh, as it rippled to the rhythm of the hymn.

It is most difficult to suppress laughter, and I failed miserably. What started as a muffled snort broke into a choked gurgle, and ended as a full-throated cough, as I strove hard to contain my mirth.

A quick look to my left, I caught the baleful eye of Frank Dover glowering at me. He must have wondered what he had brought into the church that morning, and it's not surprising that the invitation to accompany his wife and himself to church was not repeated on future occasions.

It wasn't the most auspicious start to my spell in Ireland, and the drive back to my hotel was conducted in something less than cordial warmth.

'Onward Christian Soldiers' has never been the same to me since. I can picture the incongruous scene, the disapproving look on the M.D.'s face, the generous proportions of the organist – and I still laugh to myself!

Unfortunately, that was not the only time we didn't see eye to eye. I had another bone of contention with Frank Dover. From the beginning of my working at the mill, Frank made it perfectly clear that, as mill manager, I ought to keep myself away from places where I might bump into some of the employees – that just seemed to sum up for me how backward-looking and narrow-minded he was. Anyway, it was advice I quickly chose to ignore.

The 'Railway Hotel', where I was staying, was run by a young couple at that time – John Ruane and his wife. He and I became firm friends, and we'd many a good laugh together.

One of the things about working away from home and in a new environment is getting to know the place, the people who you're working with, and the people you're going to meet outside work. I'd had my tea one evening shortly after I'd begun working in Ireland, and I turned to John.

"John, I know you've got a good bar here in the hotel, but I'd like to sample a bit of the local nightlife. Is there a good bar in the town?"

He laughed.

"A bar? We must have at least forty!" he exclaimed.

Something of an exaggeration, I suspect, but, in truth, that was typical of an Irish town. There'd be, say, twenty houses, perhaps twenty shops, and there'd be thirty-odd bars; each shop would have a bar, and every other house would have a bar.

Consequently, shops opened when the proprietors felt like opening. In other words, if you wanted to get a loaf of bread before ten or eleven in the morning, the shops wouldn't be open, because everyone was still in bed. On the other hand, if you wanted a slice of bacon at one in the morning, the chances were they'd still be open, because every shop had its own bar, and you'd get a pint of Guinness whilst they were cutting your bacon. It was a marvellous system, rather quaint, and something I'd never seen before. It certainly had advantages.

"There's the main bar in the centre of the town," said John. "You'll be OK there. There's a ceilidh band tonight, and dancing – and it's a good pint of Guinness."

"That sounds great!" I said. "Just the sort of place I'm looking for."

Unbeknown to me at the time, in the early sixties, that part of Ireland was beginning to experience an upsurge of interest in republican affairs, and, although little was heard about the IRA and terrorism, there were distant rumblings about the union of the north and south. One or two militants, even, in and around the area, which was not far from the border, had made their presence felt, and their voices heard. I found out later that the local doctor, and some local councillors, had been in prison for being members of the IRA. I didn't know this at the time. I didn't even suspect there were republican feelings in the town – I was just out to enjoy myself.

A short walk from the hotel brought me to the bar that John had recommended. Inside, the atmosphere was thick with smoke; there were people chatting, laughing, singing and dancing, as the ceilidh band thumped out an Irish jig. You felt the rhythm through the floorboards, as men and women tapped their feet to the beat, and heard it echo to the clapping of many hands. This was just the sort of place I was looking for, and a chance to meet the local people – despite what Frank Dover had told me. I knew I could enjoy this evening.

I watched for a while and then sauntered into the back room, feeling relaxed now, and enjoying the atmosphere of the place. Suddenly, a sight met my eyes that jolted me abruptly out of my genial haze.

What I saw took my breath away. There on the back wall was a mural depicting the Irish Patriots taking the Post Office in Dublin, and the Irish wiping their muddy feet on the Union Jack. I was dumbstruck, and stood looking for a while in utter amazement.

"Now, then, sor, what will you be having?"

A voice with a strong Irish accent to the side of me. My first reaction was: how do I speak? If they find out I'm from Yorkshire, they'll probably have my guts for garters.

"A... a... a pint of Guinness, please," I blurted out.

I needn't have worried. They didn't care whether I was from Yorkshire or China. Within a short space of time, I was enjoying myself in their company, listening to the music, swapping experiences and stories, as if I'd been there years. They were just as intent on enjoying an evening out as I was, and, as much as I can remember, I had a helluva time that night! They couldn't have made me feel more welcome.

The Irish, to me, couldn't have been more hospitable and pleasant, and their manner exudes a kind of easy charm that makes them good company, night or day. But, if the people were welcoming, the same could hardly be said for the main street.

This street was just like any other high street – except that it seemed to be permanently dug up for repairs. Most other high streets I've come across get dug up only when the local council workers have just finished re-surfacing it. But this one was in a constant state of chaos.

You'd walk up and down the street without any bother, but, if you wanted to cross it, that was a different matter. Occasionally, they'd put boards across the trenches that had been dug so that you could walk the plank to cross over. Where there were no boards, it was a case of scrambling over a pile of soil, leap the trench and clamber up another heap of soil – no mean accomplishment.

Eventually, I became curious.

"John," I said, one evening, as we were drinking in the hotel's bar, "there never seems to be anyone working on the street – at least, I've never seen anyone working on it when I've passed."

"Ah, no," he replied, "you won't have. They had some money to do some repairs to the services, but, after they'd started digging the road up, they found they hadn't the money they thought they had, so they stopped. It's been like that ever since, and heaven knows when they'll get the money to put it right. It's become a bit of a problem."

I can't say that that situation was typically Irish; it could happen anywhere nowadays.

It was bad enough to cross when the weather was dry; when it rained, it became a quagmire; when it was Market Day, it was a nightmare.

Once a month, to be in Killymart on market day was an unforgettable experience. All the farmers from the local hamlets used to drive into town with their sheep and cattle for the market. The place buzzed with activity. But the main street took the brunt of this seething mass; there was cow dung, and sheep muck and horse droppings all over the place, and, when it rained – as it often did – the road became awash with a river of evil-smelling brown slurry, which mixed with the mud of the dug-up road. It was not a pretty sight, and what stuck, limpet-like, to the soles of one's shoes, was a rare mixture indeed!

One of the oddest features of this monthly jamboree was the way in which the sheep followed their owners around. It was accepted without comment that, if a farmer went into a bar for a drink, a couple of sheep would follow him, and stand beside him until he was ready to leave. At that point, he would, as like as not, bundle them into the back of his car, and set off for home with a couple of sheep surveying the scene out the back windows.

Not far away was Croagh Patrick mountain, the scene of so many pilgrims climbing the mountain each year. But closer to hand was a little island set in the middle of Loch Dear. It was about ten miles from Killymart, and, at certain times of the year, every few weeks, pilgrims would come from all over Ireland to make a pilgrimage to the shrine on this island. Not being a Roman Catholic myself, I never fully understood what it was about. Perhaps I couldn't see the importance and the significance of what they were doing.

However, the idea was for the pilgrims to cross to the island, and to fast for a period of twenty-four hours. They used to take off their shoes and socks and walk around the island to the shrine, returning when they had done their penance, and arrive back at the hotel to await midnight and the end of their fast.

As it happened, the 'Railway Hotel' was the staging-post for their pilgrimage, and it got to be something of an event to have a party of pilgrims staying in the hotel.

John would say, "We've got another band of pilgrims coming this afternoon. It's all hands to the pump tonight."

This party would be additional to the one already accommodated. What used to happen was that a coach would draw up outside the hotel about four in the afternoon, and thirty or forty pilgrims of all ages would make their way into the hotel. These were pilgrims on their way to the island.

Their fast did not begin until midnight, and what they used to do was to stay at the hotel overnight, and set out for the island early the next morning. There they would stay till late into the afternoon, returning, then, to the hotel to await the end of their period of fasting at midnight.

From the moment the pilgrims entered the hotel at teatime, there was pandemonium. This was a time for celebration – and they certainly knew how to celebrate! Young or old, they were in the bar knocking back drink at a fair rate; at table, eating whatever was put in front of them; on the stairs, racing up and down in an endless chase; in each other's bedrooms, shouting, singing, screaming in fits of laughter, so that the hotel rocked with the noise of these cavorting pilgrims throughout the evening.

At the stroke of midnight came the transformation. An eerie silence descended suddenly on the bar, the dining room, the stairs, the bedrooms. It was as if someone had drawn a curtain over the scene. The fast had begun.

Morning came. There was hardly a sound as the pilgrims filed solemnly out of the hotel and into the coach. When all were aboard, the coach pulled away and disappeared down the road, heading towards the island. The hotel resumed its usual character, and everything became 'normal' again.

The 'normality', however, would last precisely half a day, for, by mid afternoon, the party of pilgrims who had already visited the island were on their way back. Exactly as the pilgrims who had departed in the morning, this party filed solemnly out of the bus and into the hotel. There was scarcely a sound; conversation was muted, and there was an air of gloom and seriousness around that was positively funereal.

Back now in the hotel, the weary pilgrims, reflecting on the gravity of their calling, sat about the place, reading silently, communicating in whispered tones, or gazing out of the window towards the distant island, with a look as vacant as a handless clock.

Every few moments, one or other would glance at his or her watch, then look away, as if in disbelief. In this situation, minutes were like hours, and hours like days. The time, indeed, 'was short, but the waiting was long'!

In the back room, meanwhile, John and his wife were busy. For them, by contrast, it was a race against the clock. Forty pilgrims were hungry, and, when midnight came, it would be all hands to the pump, just as he'd said. The feast had to be ready, or there would be a riot.

As the final hour approached to end their fast, there came a change in the atmosphere. Conversation picked up, there was a lot of to-ing and fro-ing, a bustle of activity, the occasional laugh, as the pilgrims sensed the coming of the end. Faustus himself would have been pleased at the apparent length of the hour to midnight.

The eagerly-awaited moment arrived. Instantly, there was a chaotic rush to the tables set out with food and drink. There was laughing and joking, pushing and scrambling, as each pilgrim, in turn, sought to break the fast, and resume the normality of everyday life.

If there was a party in from the island, it was a recognised hazard of the 'Railway Hotel' accommodation that you would never sleep from midnight to six in the morning. Like a déjà vu experience, pilgrims were in the bar, knocking back drink, as though drink were going out of fashion; they were eating their way through platefuls of sandwiches and pies; they were on the stairs, chasing up and down, and into each other's bedrooms.

You've never seen a happier, noisier, more boisterous mob in your life, and right throughout the night the revelry continued unabated, until exhaustion took its final toll, and peace would descend again on the hotel, just as the sun began to peer above the horizon. It was always a night to remember.

As for me, I used to stay up to watch the party who were 'living it up' until midnight – I wouldn't have minded watching those who carried on after midnight, except that I had to be up early for work in the morning.

To say that I enjoyed myself is an understatement. I met some super people, and it was a laugh a minute to see how some of these pilgrims let their hair down.

I often wondered what Chaucer would have made of them. They came from all walks of life, and I'm sure every one of them had a tale or two to tell. Maybe there were no pardoners or knights, but I could recognise a 'prioress', with her pretentions to gentility, not to mention a 'wife of Bath' who would have been quite happy, I'm sure, to 'make a man' of one or two of the assembled 'goodly company'. As a cross-section of humanity, the modern pilgrims are no less interesting than were their counterparts nearly six hundred years ago.

There was one particular occasion, however, when the laugh was well and truly on me. As I say, I couldn't really appreciate the importance of these pilgrimages in the lives of these people, but for John, the hotel proprietor, a devout Roman Catholic, they became an important part of his life and, indeed, of his living.

One particular lunchtime – I used to come back to the hotel for my lunch, the mill being just a stone's throw away – John came to me.

"Keith," he said, "would you mind doing me a favour?"

"If I can."

"We've a party coming in this afternoon. I really need every bed I've got. Could I borrow your room for just the one night?"

"No problem!" I answered.

"If you wouldn't mind, you can sleep in my mother's house – there's nobody in it and my wife and I will be sleeping there when we've got them all bedded down here."

I didn't mind in the least. I knew that the house next door, which had formerly belonged to John's mother before she died, would be OK. I wasn't thrilled, mind you. The house itself could have been Morticia's Mansion from the outside – a sprawling, gaunt, grey, Victorian edifice that would have suited admirably as the setting for a 'Tales of The Unexpected' film – or, even, a Hammer House of Horror!

"Don't worry about your stuff," he said. "I'll get all you need."

"Just a couple of shirts, and my shaving gear'll be enough," I replied.

So I left him to do that for me.

I returned to the hotel at teatime. The place was beginning to liven up already with the new intake.

I'd got so well in, as it were, that I used to go to the freezer to pick a steak for myself, put it on one side where John would know it was mine, and have it ready for me by the time I'd showered and changed. It was a good arrangement. And in the evening, if John were nowhere to be found, I'd go behind the bar, pour myself a drink, and leave the money in the till.

After my meal, this particular evening, I thought I'd watch, and mingle with, the pilgrims. It provided me with good entertainment, and there were some real 'characters' in this party.

The evening passed quickly, and I had been drinking steadily for some time – so much so that I nearly fell off the high bar stool where

I had spent most of the evening. That was sufficient indication to me that I'd had enough that evening.

At midnight, all went serious and quiet, as usual. It was then that I remembered I was not sleeping in the hotel, but next door at Morticia's Mansion.

"Where did you say I was staying?"

"Through the front door, up the stairs, and first bedroom on the left. I've put your shirts and shaver in there."

"Thanks, John. Goodnight."

And, with unsteady legs, I made my way out of the bar, down the darkened street and up the path of John's mother's house. By this time I was not seeing too well. Only a faint glimmer of light enabled me to find the door.

Everything was silent. There was not a sound. I leaned against the heavy door, and pushed it open.

A musty, damp smell greeted me – obviously the house had not been lived in for quite some time.

I felt for the light switch in what I took to be the hall, but could not find it. It was pitch black. I groped my way to where John had told me the stairs were, and found the first step.

Believing now I didn't need the lights to find my way to my bedroom, I slowly and unsteadily ascended the stairs. My shoes sent a hollow echo round the hall and landing as I carefully stepped up each tread.

There was something about this place I didn't care for.

I wasn't at all happy. It was quite weird; I had the feeling that, in the darkness, I was being watched.

Still peering down to 'see' where I was going, I turned a corner on the stairs.

Unknown to me then, all good Catholic homes have a figure of the Madonna, usually placed in the hall. This home had a ten foot high Madonna on a ledge half way up the stairs. It was lit by a single candle.

I suddenly looked up, and, in my drunken state, I saw this figure gazing down at me.

"God'streuth!" I exclaimed, and fell back two or three steps, only catching hold of the bannister which prevented my falling any further.

I set off up the rest of the stairs, past the Madonna, as though I'd been shot, turned left at the top, threw open the door of what I took to be my bedroom, and switched on the light.

Forty or more pairs of eyes were looking back at me. I nearly died on the spot. The eyes were those of figures of Madonnas scattered throughout the room. I think, in that instant, I must have aged twenty years!

A large picture of the Bleeding Heart rested over the fireplace. Coming suddenly face to face with that lot, and my heart still pumping fifty to the dozen from the unexpected encounter with the Madonna on the stairs, I sat down, pale and puffing, on the end of the bed.

Steadying myself as best I could, I looked around the array of Madonnas. There was no way I would sleep with these figures gazing at me, so I spent the next ten minutes putting them all under the bed – and that was all I remember of that night. I must have fallen asleep very quickly.

Next morning, I tried to remember where all the figures had been placed so that I could return them there without John wondering what I'd been doing the night before. I reckon the pilgrims and myself both had a headache that morning, but I would have the edge on them, in that I, at least, had been moved by a religious experience!

It was whilst I was over in Ireland that our daughter Joanne was born. I remember getting the phone call telling me I was a father – and in all my travels, I have never felt so far from home. I wanted to be there with them.

I received a letter from Philippa a couple of days later, telling me that she'd be coming out of hospital on the following Saturday. So I went to see Frank Dover.

I told Frank that I'd become a father.

"Oh, very good, very good."

He said it with as much interest and enthusiasm as he could muster - which was not very much. Not that it ever was.

"Would you mind if I took time off to go across to see them? Philippa's coming out of hospital on Saturday."

He looked up from his work for a moment.

"Right, lad. Well, today's Thursday. I don't see why you shouldn't have tomorrow afternoon off, provided you're back here for Monday morning."

He resumed his work. I couldn't believe what I'd heard. He was giving me just half a day to fly home, see Philippa and our baby, and be back here again for Monday morning. It was absurd – and uncharitable – and it was the last straw. That was it, for me.

It came at the end of a catalogue of this man's shortcomings and it was then that I realised that he was not the man with whom I wanted to spend the rest of my working life.

That Friday, at lunch time, I went back to the hotel, told John of my decision to pack the job in, put my belongings in my cases, and, with some regret at losing the friendship of John and his wife, I caught the bus back to Dublin, and the plane to Yeadon Airport. By evening, I saw our child for the first time, and Philippa, and knew I was where I wanted to be.

The following morning I went to the mill over in Potterton where I knew I would find Joe Thompson. Joe was the one who had hired me; I felt Joe should be the first to know that I wasn't going back. Frank Dover could wait.

"I know what you're going to tell me," said Joe, as I sat there in his office. "Reading between the lines, I gathered you weren't happy over there."

I told him my side of the story. He listened attentively.

"Well," he said, after a while, "it's rather strange. I don't quite know what goes wrong, but we don't seem to be able to keep our managers over there for very long. It's very odd."

I think I could have told him – but what was the point?

CHAPTER 3

For the first time in my life, I was out of work; I was on the dole, and it wasn't a pleasant feeling, especially now that there were three of us. It's a wretched situation to be in and anyone who says otherwise has never experienced what it's like.

You get up in a morning, and you've nowhere to go in order to earn your keep. There's a sense of frustration, of not knowing what you can be doing to help yourself more. If the jobs aren't there, then they're not there, and wishing won't put it right.

On more than one occasion, I wished I hadn't been so quick to pack the job in at Killymart, but, then again, when I'd thought about it a bit more, I knew I'd made the right decision.

Time passed, and there was still no work. Then, out of the blue, came Brian Porter.

I'd met Brian Porter at one or two Textile meetings some time earlier. One winter evening, there was a knock on the door, and, when I opened it, there stood the tall figure of Brian. I was taken completely by surprise.

"Now, then, Keith, am I going to freeze on your doorstep, or are you going to invite me in for a cup of tea?"

"Come in, Brian," I said. "The kettle's on."

"How're you getting on, then?" he enquired, as I led him into the lounge. He knew the answer before he'd even asked. It's just one of those things people say.

"Fine," I replied. "Well, we're OK, anyway. You know that I'm out of a job?"

"Yes; I knew that. Well, first things first. I've come to invite Philippa and yourself to the Textile Dinner."

I looked at him for a moment.

"That's very kind of you," I said, "but we don't have..."

"Listen. Don't worry. You're coming as my guests. And the next thing is, I want you to come and see me down at the mill tomorrow morning. OK?"

I nodded.

The conversation shifted to other things, and he left soon after he'd finished his cup of tea.

The following morning I went down to the mill, as instructed.

It was a Victorian, stone-built mill, with a tall chimney that dominated the skyline, its top almost scraping heavy grey clouds that scudded along.

I was shown into a Victorian-looking office, and was introduced to a tall, un-Victorian-looking gentleman. This was Brian's partner in the mill – Bill Lister. Together, as I was soon to find out, they ran the mill, and ran it in the way that a mill should be run.

"Mornin', Bill," said Brian, cheerily. "I've brought this young man to have a word with you. Do you think he could help us run the Blending Department and the raw materials?"

I sat down, and the three of us had a long chat about what I'd done and what I knew, and, at the end of it, Bill said to me, "Right, lad, the job's yours, if you want it."

Opportunity had knocked again, and was never more welcome than at that time. I accepted gladly and thankfully.

And so I went to work for two of the gentlemen of the trade, two of the best people anyone could ever hope to work for. We used to call them 'Bill and Ben', but I count myself lucky to have known them. Those days at Thomas Appleyard's Mill were the happiest days of my life.

Just for the record, Appleyard's Mill, I suppose, was as typical a Yorkshire woollen mill as you're likely to find anywhere in the region. It was built in 1897 and had been added to through the years. Consequently it had become a mixture of old stone-built sections surrounding a more modern brick-built office block in the centre of the complex.

The original owner of the mill had lived in an imposing double-fronted stone house that stood partly on the main road and partly on a track that led to the mill. This track brought you to the gates of the mill, through which, on the right, you could see the Sample Room, and Bill, as often as not, examining the various deliveries of wool.

Bill had been a tank commander at El Alamein. I said he was impressive to look at, but he was impressive in everything he said and did. He was a wonderful chap to talk to, and one of the very good reasons why the Allied Forces came out on top in the Desert Campaign in the last war. He didn't waste words, and he didn't waste people's time, but he knew what he wanted – and what he wanted, he usually achieved.

Bill had been at the mill practically all his working life apart from the war, that is – and, from what I could gather, he'd been given a pretty rough time of it. Whoever had been in charge, whether his father or his uncle, they'd treated him harshly; they had, literally, 'put him through the mill'.

Entry to his office was via a wide hallway, decorated with ornate plasterwork on the ceiling. Facing a door in the hallway hung a painting of Bill's uncle, and no one, under any circumstances, was allowed to take down or touch this picture.

There was an occasion when it was decided that the hall should be re-decorated, and it so happened that, just as a young lad, the decorator's apprentice, was about to remove the picture, Bill came bursting in through the door from the corridor, saw what he was about to do, and shouted, "Don't you touch that. That stays where it is!"

The lad looked suitably puzzled.

"But we shall need to take it down to paint the wall!" he exclaimed.

"There's no way that that picture comes off the wall. You'll have to paint round it."

The young lad looked from Bill to the painting, then back again at Bill, then with a shrug of his shoulders shuffled out into the corridor, intent, presumably, on receiving further instructions to cope with this turn of events.

I was standing in the doorway of the Blending Office at the time, listening to this. Bill turned round and noticed me. He could see that I was just as puzzled as the young lad. He came over to me, put one hand on my shoulder, and pointed at the picture with the other.

"When I took over here," Bill explained, "I made up my mind. No one is going to move that painting. That picture is a picture of my uncle. He used to think he was lord of all he surveyed, and he didn't half let me know it – every day of his working life. Well, I've put him there, right opposite the Gents, and he can look at those toilets for as long as I'm here, and let him survey that lot!"

He laughed as he said it, but I could tell that there were years of suppressed anger behind what he said. He must have gone through quite a lot in his early days.

There was another occasion when Bill enjoyed a joke. It was his own fault really.

He used to work in an old brown coat and brown boots, and anybody who met him would have taken him for just one of the employees – a caretaker or lab technician. It had to happen, sooner or later, that someone did just that.

A salesman called one day and said to Bill's secretary that he wished to speak to the managing director, though he had made no prior appointment to do so.

This particular salesman was obviously keen to get on with the day's business and make as many calls as possible. The secretary asked him to take a seat, and said she would enquire whether Mr Lister was available.

A few minutes went by, and it was obvious this salesman was not enjoying the delay.

He tapped on the office window.

"Excuse me," he said, with an air of importance. "It's getting rather late. I do take it that he knows I'm here?"

The secretary said she'd put out a call for the M.D. He was somewhere in the mill.

At that moment, Bill came from a side door – he'd been over in the Blending Department and was up to his ears in dust and grime. He nodded and smiled at the salesman, as he was walking past.

"Everything alright?" Bill asked. He was about to add that he would be with him in a moment, when the salesman butted in, and said, very annoyed, "Not really. I've been waiting to see your managing director for the best part of quarter of an hour. I'm fed up with waiting."

Bill nodded, sympathetically.

"Well, they're busy people, you know. Everybody wants things doing yesterday these days."

"I don't know about that. They're all the same these people; they sit in their offices, supping coffee all day. They don't realise that our time's just as important as theirs."

Bill looked at him for a moment, and then replied, "Ah, quite. I'll just pop in and see if he's available yet – see if he's finished his coffee."

He went into his office, took off his coat, put on his jacket, walked out again, and said to the salesman, "Now, then, how can I help you?"

The look on the salesman's face said it all. He didn't know where to put himself – nor did he make any sales that day. We never saw him again, hardly surprisingly.

It's a hard life, selling. I came to know that fact only too well in later years. You've got to know your job, but you've got to know people even better.

There was also an occasion when the firm bought a new blender/packing machine, which automatically packed the wool from the Blending Department, and this machine was Bill's pride and joy.

The machine was later adapted, but, when it was installed, it had a cage at the top, and you could actually take the side of the cage off and clean inside.

Of course, in such a condition, it was very dangerous; there were rollers which take the wool into the bale through some nip rollers, and, at that time, the manufacturers had failed to put a 'stop motion' on it. That meant that you could take the side off and put your hand in whilst the machine was in operation.

I was in the blending room next door when I heard this sudden outburst of screaming. I dashed out of the room, and on to the shop floor. There, at the end of one of the new machines, was a man with his arm caught up to the elbow in the machine, screaming blue in the face. If he'd been doing what he should have been doing, the problem would never have arisen, but the young chap had been playing around in the guts of the machine whilst it was still operating.

While I was shouting to one of the others to phone for an ambulance and the fire brigade, believing they would have to smash the machine to get the man out, Bill came running in, saw what had happened, went back for his bag of tools that he always kept in his office, and came dashing back in.

"What in heaven's name were you doing, man, to get caught in my machine – and give up shouting, give up making such a row."

It must have been extremely painful for the man.

"Don't worry," shouted Bill, above the noise of the man's screams. "It won't be long before I have you out of here."

And with that, he jumped on the machine, all six foot six of him, and began tugging at bits of the machine to loosen the retaining nuts.

Bill had been working at the machine for what seemed no more than a couple of minutes or so when in strode a burly fire officer, axe in hand. How the fire brigade had managed to get there so quickly was a mystery. But this man was ready and obviously very willing to do to Bill's machine all that was necessary to release the hapless fellow from its clutches.

Bill looked up and saw him.

"You come anywhere near my machine," shouted Bill, still trying to be heard above the now-hoarse cries of the victim, "and I'll wrap that bloody thing round your neck, do you hear?"

To his credit, the fire officer readily recognised that here was a situation that called for diplomacy rather than brute force, and immediately and very smartly took two steps back. He stood by, as helpless as the rest of us. Two or three more officers joined us, but we remained mere witnesses to the event, apart from trying to comfort the injured man.

It didn't take long for Bill to loosen the final nut that enabled the man to withdraw his arm, and he was carried off to receive attention.

It was a nasty business, but, fortunately, as I heard later, the chap suffered no permanent damage.

It would be pretty rare nowadays for something like this to happen, but in those days safety was not always top of the agenda, and that was not the only accident I saw happen in the mills. Some machines are foolproof, but not all of them are bloody-fool proof.

On a much lighter note, the highlight of our year at that time was our trip to the Carpet Show, which used to be held each year at Earl's Court. For all of us, Departmental Managers and Assistants, it used to be one of the great events of the year, and we used to look forward to it with keen anticipation. It made a change from the normal routine, and both Brian and Bill thought that it was important that we should all get together for one day in the year, away from the mill, and talk about things.

So, for one day in the year, we all used to meet at Wakefield Station, catch the train to London, and enjoy ourselves.

The carding engineer at the mill was an amiable fellow, but he didn't have a hair on his head; he was as bald as a badger, and we'd always known him as such.

The first time we went on the train down to Earl's Court was an occasion we didn't forget for quite some time; we couldn't believe our eyes when we came on to the platform, and there was this same carding engineer with a most beautiful head of bright ginger hair, which he smoothed every now and again with an elaborate flourish of his hand.

I suppose he could have got away with it – after all, many men pay the earth to improve their appearance, if they can – but, unfortunately, the piece didn't fit; it stood proud of its surroundings, as if a hedgehog had climbed on to a football. We couldn't contain our mirth, we couldn't keep our faces straight; and the more we tried to hide our laughter and sniggers, the more obvious became the object of our childish glee. We had to keep our faces steadfastly turned away for fear of bursting into howls of laughter. He was a sight to behold, especially when gusts of wind rushed along the platform, threatening to dislodge the hairpiece from its precarious moorings.

The carding engineer, all the while, remained stonily contemptuous of our antics, impassive and unmoved by such shows of immaturity. He would turn away, gaze intently down the track, and, casually running his hand along the side of his head, would again smooth down an errant lock of his ginger wig.

In future times, in jest, whenever an occasion arose when we wished to show contempt for someone, we adopted a parody of the carding engineer's gesture, extravagantly and dramatically smoothing down our hair, as we flounced out of the room in mock annoyance. It was cruel, I know, but the gesture was widely appreciated round the mill by my colleagues, and no malice intended.

It remained a common amusement for quite some time afterwards.

After that occasion, we used to see him at social functions quite regularly, still sporting his wig, and we still continued to think it peculiar, but that in no way prevented him from carrying on as he thought fit – and quite rightly, too. The wig stayed, and, in time, we hardly gave it a second glance.

Rather strangely, however, and in similar fashion, there used to be a chap called John Dickinson, who was the dyehouse manager, and, throughout his time there, he became almost a byword for being the untidiest, shabbiest person in the region; he wore a grubby coat that was covered in green dye, and where there was no green dye, there was red dye. At least, he was colourful.

But what a transformation on the day of the annual trip! Pinstripe suit, bowler hat, polished black shoes, and tightly furled umbrella – he was the epitome of sartorial elegance! We stared in disbelief, as he stood there on the grimy, windswept platform, for all the world looking like a City Gent. Even Brian and Bill would see the funny side of this metamorphosis in the figure of the scruffiest employee in the mill.

At the Show itself at Earl's Court, we kept losing him, but every now and again we'd catch sight of him at a stand, with crowds of hopeful dealers plying him with more and more wine, in the fervent hope and expectation of plenty from him. I don't know whether he managed to obtain any orders, but he was certainly a very good 'con' artist, and looked every inch the part of a wealthy mill owner in town for business.

Incidentally, it was this worthy gentleman who decided to stand as prospective Tory candidate for a seat on the Council. He was the thinking man's dyehouse manager, energetic, and with ambitions to rise in the community and serve it as best he may.

We were not quite sure how he managed it, but, somehow, he talked a group of us at the mill into canvassing for him, in the run-up to the local election.

What we had failed to take into account, when we'd promised to assist, was the area where this help was to be given. As he was a new boy to politics, the Tory selectors had given him the worst area of the Borough to contest – as we all soon found out.

On the first evening we were to canvass for John, I drove to the middle of a particular housing estate in the heart of his constituency, where John had asked me to start.

The number of children, dogs, broken fences, litter and a sprinkling of torn and filthy mattresses lying in the privet hedges, should have given me a clue. A canvasser for a Tory candidate here was about as welcome as a dead rat – except that one of the latter would have been seen probably far more frequently than one of the former in this locality. At least I would have rarity or novelty value I thought.

I sat there for a moment, surveying the scene, like a General, estimating the battleground – the comparison is not too fanciful, except that I was no General.

Several youths, on the other side of the road from where I parked the car, were fooling around, a couple of them smoking, one sitting on a brick wall, and others lounging around, occasionally aiming a kick or a punch at each other. They looked bored to death. Without wishing to pre-judge a situation, I felt that here my car might well receive unwelcome attention.

Standing close by, two girls, in their early teens I would have guessed, were practising their new-found charms from beneath their heavy mask of make up. Their shrill laughter pierced the air from time to time, followed by giggling, and sly glances at one of the boys. For them, this charade was not play; they were playing a more serious game.

I got out of the car, making sure I'd locked it, and put the aerial down. I peered over a hedge into the garden of the first house. A child's toy pram, a tricycle, two pairs of yellow wellingtons and a plastic spade were strewn about what might have been, sometime, a lawn.

I was careful to close the remnant of the wooden gate behind me, and strode purposefully up to the faded green front door.

From within, sounds of a baby crying, a man's voice, shouting, and a dog barking were not inviting. My resolution wavered slightly; I tapped faintly on the door, hoping that no one would hear, so that I might move on to the next house.

The knocking was greeted with a blood-curdling bellow from some massive hound that was already chewing the screws out of the other side of the door, as it tried to get to me. I retreated smartly. A fleeting memory of *The Monkey's Paw* briefly came to mind.

This violent eruption was followed by a scuffle, and curses, as someone dragged back the hound from the door. A bolt was drawn back, a key turned in the lock, and the door opened slightly.

A glowering pair of eyes looked down on me – a scruffy-looking man, in a scruffy-looking pair of jeans, and a scruffy-looking T-shirt, grunted something which may have been, "What do you want?"

His knee was jamming the unseen hound against the back of the door.

"Good evening, sir," I said, trying to sound convincing and confident. "I am canvassing on behalf of Mr John Dickinson, your prospective Conservative candidate. May we count on your support?"

I didn't quite catch the words the man uttered, but I got the general drift. In the moments that followed, I even surprised myself. I was down that drive, over the remnant of the gate, on to the pavement and back inside the car, before the hound had even got out of the door.

My hasty retreat brought forth a spontaneous burst of applause from one or two of the gang who had watched the drama with some interest from across the street! I wasn't quite sure whether the applause was for my speed and agility, or my hurdling technique over the tricycle, wellingtons, pram and gate. Through the closed car window, I could hear loud guffaws from across the road.

Having regained a little of my composure, I thought it prudent not to pursue this canvassing activity any further. I drove off, smiling cheerfully at the youths, as they paused in their uproarious laughter to give me a V-sign farewell. Not the most successful venture I've ever undertaken.

Needless to say, that put a quick end to any ideas I may have entertained about entering the political arena. I did try one or two houses further around the estate, but I felt that my input into this territory was less than adequate. Others had experienced much the same as I had.

John tried to hold us to our promise to help him, but there was no way we were going to face the wrath of the electorate in that area. Such activities are best left to those capable of dealing with rabid dogs and disillusioned voters. I know my limitations.

We used to have visitors to the mill. One such visitor was an official from the Wool Board. When we knew that this very important gentleman was coming, Brian asked me if I would accompany the official and himself when they toured the building. I was very pleased to do so.

The day came and we began a tour of the different departments, and met the operatives as they worked at their machines. This official seemed quite impressed, and we stopped at one machine to inspect it more closely.

"Oh, I like that," said the official, turning with a smile to Brian. "It's a lovely blend of wool," he commented.

Now, if you're a textile man, the one thing that you know is the difference between things that are wool, and things that are not – and this was not; Brian and I knew that this was 100% acrylic.

So much for highly important officials – if they can't tell the difference between wool and acrylic, how do they become highly important officials? Suffice to say, I caught Brian's glance, a look of total disbelief registered there which spoke volumes. I disappeared into an office to have a good laugh, and save the official from embarrassment – he probably never knew of his blunder. Even high and important officials are not always perfect.

In those days, Thomas Appleyard's was quite a big mill and gave steady employment to a lot of people, though the pay was not excessive.

At the time I was there, my sister had started courting a young man who, to put it bluntly, was wealthy. To such an extent that he owned a race horse. You are seriously wealthy if you have the money to own your own race horse. Well, that may not be true in some areas, but where I come from in Yorkshire, it definitely is true.

The horse itself was not noted for having achieved anything special – not having achieved anything at all, to be truthful. But one day my sister said to me, "Keith, Pensa is running at Haydock Park next Wednesday afternoon. If you want to put some money on, it's a fair bet to win."

I've never been a gambling man, and wouldn't know one end of a horse from the other – well, hardly – but I thought, "Why not? If it wins, it's a bit of a bonus, and we could do with a little extra." So I decided, if I could find the time, to put a few bob on this unknown outsider called Pensa.

I happened to be walking through the mill the following day when I bumped into the assistant foreman, and we chatted for a while.

Just as we were going our separate ways, I remembered he was a chap who liked a little flutter now and again, so I said to him very quietly, "By the way, I've got a little tip for you, if you're interested."

He said he was.

"My sister's got this boyfriend who owns a horse. It's called Pensa, and it's running in the 2.30 at Haydock Park next Wednesday. It's an outsider, but I understand quite a few people are fancying it. It might be worth a bob or two on it."

If I'm honest, I think there might have been an element of boasting in my revelation to him – letting him know, for example, that my family had these wealthy connections.

"Great!" he exclaimed. "Thanks, Keith. Well done, lad."

"You'll keep it to yourself, won't you?" I said, suddenly realising that I didn't really want him to be building this thing up to be bigger than it was.

"'Course I will – don't worry about that. I won't tell a soul."

The next day I'm going through the winding shed, and all the men at the machines nod at me and grin or wink as I pass. One or two call out, "Good lad! Just the ticket!" and suchlike phrases.

Very unusual.

I thought, "What's going on here? Something's wrong."

It didn't dawn on me till I went into the carding room. There on the wall was a note in large red letters: "PENSA FOR YOUR BEER."

"What the hell... So much for keeping it to himself. Just then the carding engineer (minus hair, of course) came in.

"The whole mill's on it, Keith. We've all heard about it, and we've all put our holiday money on it. It's great news!"

"You've done what?"

"Put our holiday money on that horse."

"But, I only..."

"It isn't often we get a fair chance of a shot at something like this, you know," he interrupted. "It's absolutely great! Thanks, Keith."

I began to feel uneasy, and the feeling didn't go away any as the days passed, getting nearer to the day of the race. I think I began to understand how a condemned prisoner must feel.

Amongst the workforce, however, there was a sense of excitement in their chatter. Every time the race was mentioned, eyes would light up, and there would be an air of anticipation, like children on Christmas Eve. The more their excitement, the more my sense of foreboding.

The Wednesday of the race came. Everywhere I went, there were notices pinned up on the wall:

"PENSA TODAY!" proclaimed one huge notice.

I wanted to die – or disappear, anywhere.

What the hell's going to happen if this bloody horse doesn't win? Agitation added spice to my choice of words; panic began to take a firm grip on my throat. I felt terrible when I heard the shouts of encouragement that came to me from everyone in the mill. "Good old Keith!" was the cry. Two or three young women came up, smiling, and gave me a peck on the cheek.

"You'll do for me, lad!" said one of the old men, quietly, as he turned back to his machine, still beaming with the thought of making a bit of extra money for his family.

That lunch time, I went home for my lunch. The question was: "Do I go back, or do I keep away for a few days?" I sat and puzzled over that question through a cheerless lunch.

Eventually, I made up my mind. I had to go back, come what may, but I reckoned I'd be looking for a new job. They'd never let me forget this – how I'd let them down, how I'd cost them the money for their summer holidays. That's the least they would do. I could hardly bear to think what might happen. No use, now, trying to explain that the tip had been given more in hope than any serious expectation.

I walked slowly back to work, taking a long time, and eventually reached the mill yard. A burglar couldn't have wished to be less obtrusive.

They were all clustered round radios, as I hurried into my office and shut the door. I tried to work to take my mind off the race, but I couldn't sit still, and I couldn't concentrate.

When I stood up to look out of the window, I could still see anxious faces staring intently into space, as each of the men and women listened to one of the several radios dotted around the mill.

Down on the shop floor, the muffled sound of a race commentary competed against the throb of the machines.

How I got through the next few minutes after that, I shall never know. All I remember is that there was a strange silence, which seemed to last for ages. Suddenly, a roar went up, followed by shouting – I couldn't tell whether they were cries of joy or anger. I pushed open my door; as I did, the shouts became cheers, and more cheers, which echoed round the mill.

An unforgettable surge of relief came to me in that moment.

Pensa, as it happened, cantered home to win by six lengths. The men and women were over the moon at the thought of their winnings – and there was a grey hair on my head for every pound they'd won!

I shall never forget that wave of relief sweeping over me when I heard the news – nor the volleys of congratulations I received when I had to leave my office to go down to speak to one of the workers on the shop floor. There were tears of gladness in the eyes of some of the men and women, and these were reflected in my own eyes, which almost betrayed my relief.

What an experience! I shall never forget Pensa, that's for sure, and I bet there's plenty of workers who'll have raised their pints of beer to Pensa, as these lucky ones enjoyed their holidays in Blackpool, or Bridlington, or wherever.

Sadly, from my point of view, I completely forgot about backing the horse myself.

That same year was also the year of the Great Flood. Appleyard's, as I mentioned earlier, was a very old fashioned mill, a blend of new and old; it had been built on and raised, built on and raised for a good many years.

During my time there, an extension was planned for one of the older parts of the mill, and, when the diggers finally got started to excavate for the foundations, they unearthed a complete street, with cobbled roads, tiny brick houses, houses still with their doors intact that you could push open, and enter a world not seen for several generations.

It was a thrilling but almost uncanny sensation. To walk into houses like these was like being in a time warp – something similar to finding Pompeii again.

Of course it created a lot of interest at the time, and archaeologists and historians flocked to the mill to have their say, to record the scene, and to analyse the implications.

Our boss, however, was only interested in one thing – getting the extension done.

"I'll give you a fortnight," he said to the assembled group of historians. And a fortnight to the day, the bulldozers moved in, and that was that. So much for history. Commerce takes precedence.

That part of the mill, though, was the scene of an incident some time before the extension was started. The building was used as a warehouse for wool – great big bales stored ready for use when required.

Entry to this warehouse was down a slope which led to a tunnel that went under the main part of the mill. It was well below ground level, and going into it was, I suppose, like going down into a drift mine. At the far end were some small windows that served to let in a little light, but not much. On the other side of the windows, almost at window height, was a beck that ran past the mill.

On this particular day, the sun had shone hazily through the morning, but, by the afternoon, the atmosphere had become oppressive with a sultry, stifling heat.

About the middle of the afternoon, the sun disappeared completely behind a heavy bank of cloud, and, within minutes, rain began to fall. Once it had begun, it was obvious that it was going to come down in torrents, and it poured down for about an hour. It stopped as suddenly as it had begun, and no one took any particular notice of it, except to remark that the rain had 'cleared the air'.

The foreman, a chap by the name of Jack Thompson, was working in the mill with a young Pakistani employee – probably about sixteen or seventeen, I should think.

As he was working, the foreman happened to glance up; he looked away, and quickly looked back again. He hadn't been mistaken the first time; he realised that what he was seeing at the windows was not the sky outside, but water. It was over the top of the windows, and the effect was rather like being in an aquarium, and water was rushing by at great speed. Not only that; the windows were beginning to buckle under the pressure of water.

The only exit was via the tunnel. At the same moment that Jack shouted to the young lad to get out – he was working at the far end of the warehouse – the windows caved in with a deafening crash, and thousands of gallons of water engulfed everything in a matter of moments.

Jack turned and ran hell for leather for the tunnel, escaping into the side of the mill yard just as a wall of water heaved itself through the tunnel, raced at breakneck speed through the yard, and battered its way through the doors of the mill on the other side of the yard.

In its wake, great bales of wool were tossed around and up the tunnel, like so much flotsam. In no time, the mill was awash, and the yard was filling up with bales. It was completely flooded.

It was then that Jack realised that the young lad had not followed him out, or, if he had, had not been able to make it. His heart missed a beat, and he was seized with panic, feeling that he was responsible for the lad's safety.

There was no way back into the warehouse down the tunnel – that was under four feet of water. It seemed an odds on bet that the lad would be dead by now.

It was the works manager who then had the presence of mind to find a possible solution. Taking two or three of the men with him, he went out and ran round to the other side of the mill, to the side where the beck was still rushing down past the basement. With scarcely a word, he slipped into the water, and swam to the spot where the windows had been not ten minutes before, and where water was still gushing in through the openings.

The sight that met his gaze was unforgettable; there, floating on a bale, with no more than six inches between the bale itself on the top of the water and the ceiling of the warehouse, was one very frightened young Pakistani lad. He was spread-eagled out on top of the bale, his bony fingers sunk deep into the bale's rough sacking. His eyes were white with terror as he lay there, face down, too frightened to move in case he lost his precarious hold on the floating bale.

It took quite some time to coax the bale and the young lad near to the window space, but, eventually, he was hauled out, none the worse for his horrific experience.

The water took a while to subside from around the mill, but, within a relatively short time, things got back to normal, and the Great Flood was consigned to memory.

CHAPTER 4

About 1967, 1 began to feel the need for change once again, happy though I'd been for so many years.

The marvellous thing about knowing Brian and Bill was that, right from the start they both said, if I got the offer of a better job, all I need do was to come to tell them. Now was the time to tell them I wanted to try to move further up the ladder.

I started casting around for jobs. One day, an advertisement appeared in the *Yorkshire Post* – a mill in Scotland was requiring a mill manager. The town where this mill was situated was in an area which, for comparison's sake, could be classed as the West Riding of Scotland, though I doubt whether many Scots would appreciate this comparison.

It was at the centre of the Scottish woollen industry in the sixties, and the place was thriving.

How quickly things change. It has gone now, almost without the slightest trace of its existence – and more's the pity.

I decided to apply for the job of mill manager and was fortunate to get an interview. It was at this interview in Dewsfield I first met Jim Watson.

Jim was the M.D., a tall, heavy-looking chunk of a man. You couldn't make out whether he was Scottish, or Yorkshire, or what – he was a real mixture of everything. He'd been an officer in the Cameron Highlanders during the War. Born and brought up in Bradford, he'd spent most of his working life in Scotland. He was also very different from many of the other M.D.s I'd met in the industry; for one thing, he was a bit of a bully, and he used to get what he wanted by bullying people.

I was eventually offered the job, and so, for the next period of my life, I would get to know Scotland from the inside – the real Scotland, that is, not just the picture post card Scotland that attracts so many tourists, but the dour heart of it.

They don't come any more dour than the people of Kilavon, a smallish town not far from the west coast of Scotland.

If I say that the mill was set in an area that was not the easiest place to live, you may recognise a considerable understatement. The local people lived a harsh and very difficult life at times, and the mood of the people reflected this toughness.

There were obviously many pleasant and happy families in the estate around the mill, seeking to live a law-abiding, honest and decent existence, but it is not too much of an exaggeration to say that those seemed to be in the minority. I hasten to add that the Scots who lived there were by no means any worse than you would find in similar estates in England, Ireland or Wales, where similar conditions give rise to the same problems.

The mill itself was an old, single-storey building, almost lost to sight amongst the jumble of prefabricated houses of all shapes and sizes, situated about a quarter of a mile from the town centre, and on the edge of the housing complex – sufficiently hidden away to be out of sight and, therefore, out of mind.

A small corner shop was the only sign of commercial activity apart from the mill – and this small shop was often adorned with boarded up windows and padlocked doors; this would be the result of some earlier raid by some of the local inhabitants.

Inside the mill, it was compact and unusually modern with regard to its machinery. Everything that was necessary for a mill to be run profitably was there, except for one major factor – the chairman.

For many years it had been a family concern, but the current chairman, a charming, quietly spoken gentleman who knew much about life, had not the slightest idea how to run a mill.

It was hardly surprising that the mill had fallen into difficult financial circumstances, and, had the chairman gone on much longer in the same way, he would have lost everything. But fate sometimes steps in, and alters the scene. The 'joker in the pack', this time, was Jim Watson.

Jim had come 'out of the blue', as it were. He'd been the managing director at a mill a little further up the road. It was one of those situations where a new M.D. had come in, been given full control, had got people doing just what he wanted them to be doing, when up pops the whizz-kid son of the owner, who immediately takes over, and sets the mill back to square one. This scenario is not uncommon. It was a situation that someone like Jim Watson would not endure one moment longer than he had to.

Within a short time, Jim had struck an agreement with the chairman of the adjacent mill, offering to manage the mill as long as Jim himself was totally in control.

Jim was a good managing director, and he could make things 'go', but to be really efficient he needed a mill manager – and this was the situation I found myself in when I was lucky enough to be appointed.

It was a big move for us because it meant we had to find a house. We eventually settled on a lovely house that was being built overlooking a golf course, but we had to wait for some time before the house was completed. So I went into lodgings, as I started my new job at the Spinning Company.

I settled down quite well. I hadn't a great deal of money, but I survived. My car was a little yellow thing that shuffled around to and from the mill, like a galloping maggot.

"Is that your car out there?" Jim asked me one day. It was, I confessed.

"It's spoiling the look of the place. Can't you find somewhere to put it where people can't see it?"

Then he started laughing.

"Tell you what. Take that thing away, and I'll buy you one."

And that was how I came to have my first company car. It was a Singer Chamois, and I was really proud of it.

Of course, nobody gives money away – and certainly not Jim. He was, as I said, an out and out bully in his tactics, but, as with nearly all bullies that I've come across, if you fight them at their own game, they begin to react more reasonably. Well, some do.

However, with Jim, I soon found out that, if you didn't do things the way Jim wanted, the fur would soon begin to fly, and he would get his own way at any cost.

One Saturday morning, I went down to the mill. We'd just had some new machinery installed – new spinning frames. Something had gone wrong and there was a serious breakdown, and I was obviously worried at the loss of production. It looked as though the machines would be off line for at least a week.

I went to see the foreman.

"What are we going to do about this, then?" I asked, quite well aware that there appeared to be no immediate solution.

"Well," replied the foreman, "there's one thing we can try, if you're prepared to take the risk, that is."

"What do you suggest?"

"Up the road, at the other mill, the fitters are in at this very moment, fitting some of these new machines. Why don't you go up there and see if they'll lend us some of their spare parts to fit our machines, and then they can order some more?" It sounded a good idea to me.

"Provided one thing," added the foreman, "that Jim doesn't find out."

"What do you mean?"

"If he thinks you're borrowing anything from where he used to work, he'll go wild."

"Well," I said, "we'll just have to make sure he doesn't find out."

Without further thought, I rang their mill manager, explained the situation, and, thankfully, in no time at all, a fitter was on his way down to us with the spares we needed.

It didn't take long for our machines to be stripped down, and the spares fitted in place. Another five minutes and we would have been back in operation again.

At that moment, in walked Jim. I suppose it was just bad luck – certainly bad timing – on his part.

Surprised to see us, he spluttered, "What the hell's going on here?"

"Oh, it's OK, Jim," I said, doing my best to sound nonchalant. "We had a slight problem with one of the machines, but it's all sorted out now."

At that moment, he turned and saw the engineer from his old mill.

"What the hell are you doing here?" he asked.

"Er," he hesitated and looked at me. "We've just let you have some spares from our machines."

"Well, you can take the bloody things out again now, because we don't want them here."

And he made us take the spares out. We had to wait over a week for the replacements to come from Belgium, production was at a standstill, and I was unable to do anything about it. It was a completely wasted week.

That was Jim, though. His pride stuck to him tighter than a limpet grabs a rock. He wasn't going to be beholden to anybody, least of all to those at his old mill.

Jim always struck me as being rather odd. His regimental days had left him with a drawer full of medals which he used to like to inspect from time to time. Nothing wrong in that, I suppose, but he used to choose some odd times to inspect them, as though he had to check that his past was still in place and all was well with the world.

I never really understood him, and I didn't really know how to deal with him – perhaps that was partly my own inexperience.

There was one particular occasion when this came home to me quite vividly. It was the day before the start of the winter holiday. I'd had a particularly bad day, and a particularly bad night before it. When things went wrong at the mill, they used to ring me up through the night and I would have to get up and go down to the mill to sort it out.

On this particular day, I hadn't had much sleep, but at least, I thought, the next day is the start of the holidays.

About four in the afternoon, that day, Jim sent for me to go to his office.

"Come in, lad," he said. "Sit down."

I sat down by the side of his large desk. "How are you getting on, then?"

"Fine, Jim," I said. "We've got everything working well, and there don't seem to be any major problems."

"Good," he said. "Now, tomorrow morning..."

"It's Saturday tomorrow," I reminded him, without thinking.

"I know what day it is," he said, sharply. "Let me carry on. Tomorrow morning, I want you to come in so that we can..."

"I won't be in tomorrow morning," I said, looking him straight in the eye. "It's my holidays. I'm going on my holidays at five this afternoon."

He looked down at me as I was sitting there, and I could feel that he was going to explode any minute. His eyes narrowed and his face turned a deep red. I could feel my own hackles rising, too.

"Look, lad, you're the flaming manager of this mill, and if I want you in on Saturday morning you'll bloody well come in."

In the corner of the office was a sink, and, as he said these words, he turned away from me to wash his hands. As I sat there, at the side of the desk, I thought, "I've had enough of this, I've really had enough."

I stood up. I'd made my mind up.

"Jim," I said, doing my best to sound calm and in control, "as far as I'm concerned, you can stuff this mill where the monkey stuffs its nuts. I'm going on holiday tonight, whether you like it or not."

I stood up, glaring at him.

And, even as I was saying it, I was thinking to myself, "What are you saying to him? Oh, Lord, you're in trouble now, you fool. Just sit down and shut up."

He still had his back to me at the sink. And then he started shaking. I thought, "Is he shaking in rage?" I could see his shoulders heaving.

And then I realised that he was laughing, laughing uncontrollably. His whole big frame was convulsed with laughing; it was infectious, and I began, in spite of myself, to join him in whatever it was that was funny.

"Ee, lad," he spluttered, turning round to face me after a while, "I wondered when you were going to have a go at me. Tha's done me the world of good. Now get off on your holidays."

And still laughing to himself, he waved me away with his hand, and I beat a retreat from the office.

As I mentioned earlier, one of the problems of this particular mill was its location. It stood in the roughest and most rundown part of Kilavon and there were quite a few unsavoury characters living there, and, of course, working at the mill. It made life very difficult.

There's nothing there now – the houses are gone, and in their place is a field; the mill, too, has disappeared almost completely, apart from the tracks where the machines used to run up and down.

Nothing else remains. It was a very different kettle of fish in those days, in the mid-sixties, when it was in its heyday. It was a tough life, spent among tough people – but I have many happy memories of our time there.

You can imagine, perhaps, that, in such an area, security was one of our biggest problems. The mill was a prime target, and was frequently the object of the depredations of some of the people from thereabouts.

Eventually, I came to know an old chap - a chap who had lived on the local housing estate for many years and who was known to many of the people in the area. I gave him the job of nightwatchman. The mill, although it was in the centre of the town, was nevertheless a very isolated and quiet place at night, and I was always nervous about what went on there after dark. For this reason, then, I used to have predetermined times when I would ring up the nightwatchman just to check that everything was alright.

For one reason or another, I'm afraid I couldn't trust the people round there. One particular night comes to me like a recurring nightmare. I was sitting at home, and, as usual, decided to check up that all was in order.

I rang, but could get no response. I waited, then rang again at the next predetermined time – still no response.

I started to worry. Something, I knew, was wrong. I got up and fetched my coat.

"You're not going down there at that time of night," said Philippa. "You'll get mugged."

"I've got to see if he's alright, haven't I?" I replied. I wasn't so thrilled myself to be going down to the mill at this time of night. "Don't worry," I said to her, with rather less conviction in my voice than I had hoped for.

I set off in the car.

"What on earth am I doing?" I muttered to myself, as I drove along. "I must be barmy, doing this."

At that moment, by pure chance, a police panda car drew up alongside me at some traffic lights.

Without any further hesitation, I motioned to the policeman in the car, and he pulled over to the side of the road.

"I can't raise my nightwatchman on the phone," I said. "I'm just on my way down to see what's wrong."

"Which mill?" he asked.

I told him.

"Oh, my goodness!" he exclaimed, or words to that effect, and jumped back quickly into the car. "Just follow us."

By the time we arrived at the mill, there must have been six or eight cars pulling in, with their lights flashing.

"What the heck have I started now?" I thought to myself.

The cars screamed to a halt, and, suddenly, the place was alive with policemen. It was just like a scene from some New York gangster film. People were rushing out of their houses to see what was going on. Burly policemen were jumping out of their cars, ready to do battle in the cause of law enforcement, and you could just imagine that a gang of crooks had barricaded themselves inside the mill, with ten or fifteen hostages to protect them. They'd start shooting next...

"Have you got the key, laddie?" one of the policemen asked. He was no older than I was, but, in this situation, I wasn't arguing about such a minor point. There was no time to waste, if the crooks were not going to escape... I was getting carried away.

I opened the office door – the room was in total darkness; something was obviously wrong.

'What's going on in here?' I thought.

Several of the police charged through with me into the next room. The lights from half a dozen torches almost simultaneously merged into one beam, lighting up one solitary figure.

There, in the middle of the floor, with his hands firmly clutching an empty whisky bottle, sat the nightwatchman, absolutely pie-eyed.

"Come in and have a drink," he said, finding considerable difficulty in making the words fit the pattern that was in his head.

Half a dozen of Scotland's best young police officers stood gazing down at this figure on the floor. And the officer whose help I had enlisted a short while before turned to me, and said, "I think I'll leave the rest to you, young man. I think you've got a wee problem there."

Needless to say, I sacked the nightwatchman the following morning. But the police raid made local headline news, though I'm not sure whether the resultant publicity was welcome or not.

So, as far as security was concerned, we were back at square one.

"Where the heck am I going to find another nightwatchman?" I wondered. The following morning I talked it over with Jim.

"What are we going to do?" I said. "You know what security's like round here. Give these people even half a chance and they're in like..."

"The best thing to do," interrupted Jim, "is to get some guard dogs. Let's have some professional security men in. That'll do the trick."

And Jim sat back, pleased with his own suggestion.

So I called in a local security unit, and we agreed that, on the nights when we had no nightshift, Saturdays and Sundays, the security unit would bring two men and two dogs.

The first night, all went well; there was no problem whatsoever – all was quiet through the night. No phone call, no early panic, no wondering what more we had lost. I was obviously quite happy to let sleeping dogs lie – or whatever two ferocious, highly-trained dogs do when they're on their round! I thought, 'Well, at least we're secure for the time being.'

Somehow, though, for every well laid plan, there's a weakness, and, in this case, the weakness was Jim, the managing director. He just couldn't resist; he couldn't let people get on with their own jobs without interference, but, on this particular occasion, he came unstuck. It came about like this.

The Saturday following our first successful venture with the dogs and their handlers, Jim had taken his wife out for the evening, and, as was usually the case, through the evening, he had consumed rather more drink than was wise.

"We've got some new security down at the mill," he said to his wife. "Let's see how good they are."

And without further ado, he staggered out of the local tavern, clambered clumsily into his big Mercedes, and sped off to the mill.

Surprisingly, he was sufficiently aware of what he was doing when he reached the mill to remember that it would be unwise not to let the guards know of his presence.

"Attention, please! Attention, please!"

He had switched on the tannoy.

"This is the managing director. I repeat, this is the managing director. I am coming to speak with you."

With that, he set off into the mill.

He blundered clumsily through one door, and got half way across to the next door – he was, in other words, in a kind of no man's land when the patrolling dogs saw him. At that same moment, he saw them, and became rapidly aware of the tactical error he'd committed. He turned and set off back as best his unsteady legs would carry him, seeking the sanctuary that lay behind the closed door he had just come through.

There was an audible ripping sound that echoed round the empty mill, as the first of the dogs got a good purchase on the seat of Jim's trousers. Terror was written all over his face, as he flung open the door and made a dash for his car, this ferocious hound snapping by now at his exposed shirt tail. By the time he had gained the safe haven of his car, his trousers were round his knees, in shreds, with both dogs tearing apart the bits of severed fabric.

Two embarrassed, but concerned security men got the dogs under control again, as Jim put his foot down to leave the scene as quickly as possible. No doubt, when he had gone, they patted the dogs for a job well done, and retired to the mill to enjoy a good laugh.

When they told me, the following morning, what had happened, I could well imagine that Jim would be seeking their resignation before long; in fact, he never once referred to it.

So far as I know, Jim never again went to check on security at the mill – not that we didn't have problems, but there was no way he would venture down there again when the dogs were on patrol.

There was another thing about Jim Watson – apart from being a busybody, he was somewhat eccentric.

In order to keep pace with the modern trends in the textile industry, Jim purchased a new 'toy' for testing the moisture content present in bales of wool.

It was extremely useful to have one of these in the mill, but Jim kept it in his office and, every now and again, would take out this instrument to inspect it (in between inspecting his medals). It had two prongs on it, rather like a car aerial, and a grip and dial for making readings. The prongs were pushed into the bale of wool, and from the reading it could be assessed how much moisture was in the wool of a particular bale. Jim was fascinated with this machine.

On one occasion, the foreman happened to be in with Jim in his office when Jim's secretary came in, telling him that a certain gentleman had called to see him.

Jim's eyes lit up. He always liked to impress people.

He said to the foreman, "I know this chap. Will you do something for me? Just walk through reception and talk into this gauge as if it were a walkie-talkie. This chap's always wanted walkie-talkies in his mill. Just say something like, 'Calling Carding Department, calling Carding Department, are you receiving me? Over.' And I bet this fellow will go back to his mill and try to get the same system."

When the manager of the nearby mill (the visitor) saw the foreman walking through reception talking into the moisture gauge, he nearly split his sides with laughing. He'd had one of these gauges at his mill for some time and recognised it immediately. Knowing Jim of old, he also knew what game Jim was trying to play.

When Jim asked him what he thought of his new internal communication system, the manager said he was most impressed. Jim preened himself on his subterfuge.

"But how did you manage to convert a moisture gauge into a walkie-talkie?" he asked.

Jim, naturally, had no answer. But that didn't seem to stop him doing other equally daft things at other times later on.

Wherever you have a large number of people working in one place, you're bound to get a fair number of crooks and dodgers, if my experiences at Kilavon are anything to judge by. Times can be very hard for many people, but some of the employees at that mill just seemed to pilfer whatever they could, not from necessity, but just for the sheer hell of it.

To these people, it was a kind of life-game. If you could get away with something, literally, then it was 'one up' to you. You'd got the better of 'them'. Perhaps it was their way of protesting against the situation into which fate had unwillingly thrust them.

The nightwatchman wasn't by any means the only one I had to sack from that mill. I got a phone call one evening from Peter Mackintosh, the chap who owned the local corner shop. Over the period I'd been at the mill, I'd got on with him very well and came to know him as a good friend.

"There's a chap who works in your spinning department," he said. "He wears a big, loose-fitting raincoat, and every time he comes in here he gets fatter and fatter. I'm sure he must be pinching wool."

"Well, look," I said. "Next time he comes in, just give me a shout, and I'll be down. Thanks, Peter."

A couple of nights later, he rang again.

"My son's in the shop, serving, and there's a helluva queue. Your chap's at the back of the queue; if you ask me, he looks three months pregnant."

"Right," I said, "I'll be there in two ticks."

With that, I sped down to the shop a couple of hundred yards or so away.

There, still in the queue, stood a man whom I immediately recognised as one of our employees.

I went up to him.

"Now, then, how're you going on?" I asked, and clapped him on the shoulder. He staggered forward slightly, and, as he did so, three hanks of yarn slid from under his coat and rolled on to the floor.

If looks could have killed...!

So that was the end of another one. I think I had to sack more people from that mill than I've had to do in all my other jobs put together. It's not a nice job, but sometimes it has to be done.

Working in Scotland was a wonderful experience, and I wouldn't have missed it for anything. By and large, there are no finer people than the Scots, and, when they get to know you, their good-heartedness and generosity are hard to beat anywhere in the world.

Right from the start, Philippa and I agreed that, if we were to make our lives in Scotland, then we had to throw ourselves into whatever a Scottish community had to offer. When in Rome - or, in this case, Scotland - we'd do all we could to become part of the community.

We were buying a new house on the edge of Kilavon, right next to the golf course. It was a new estate with very pleasant, well-designed houses which we liked a great deal, and the house we'd chosen was at the head of the estate, some three or four hundred yards from the main road.

I was obviously very anxious to get settled in, so a great deal of my spare time I used to go up to the estate to chivvy the builder into getting my house finished as soon as possible.

The weather held fine enough for the builders to press on, and it was just before Christmas, 1966, that our new home was ready for us, and Philippa and I were able to move in.

Unfortunately, our home was all that was ready. We moved into what can only be described as a building site with one completed house on it, right at the far end of a cul-de-sac, and that was ours.

To get to it was a feat of tenacity and endurance in itself. If the cement-mixers didn't get you, the piles of bricks did. There were pipes and cables, rubble and bags of concrete everywhere. Our progress from the main road to our house was like some demented form of assault course, with mud the chief enemy.

The reason for mentioning this is that we were, nevertheless, glad to be there, and prepared to sample what we could of Scottish life.

Not very long, then, after moving in, I got to know Peter at the local shop pretty well. It was his part in my dealing with the wool thief that reminded me of another incident in which he was the prime mover.

I was in his shop one evening on my way home from work. We were chatting about nothing in particular when, out of the blue, he said:

"I'm a member of Round Table. We have a great time. How do you fancy joining us?"

Remembering what Philippa and I had agreed when we moved to Scotland, I thought I ought to be enthusiastic, and, indeed, the idea of being asked to join Round Table I found very flattering.

"Yes," I replied, "I'd be very interested in joining."

"Well, look," he said, "the next event is Burns' Night. We hold it in Alloway - the very village in which Burns was born - in the hotel just across the road from Burns's cottage. You can't have a more authentic Burns' Night than that."

"Fine," I said, feeling pleased that I was about to make headway into Scottish society. It was obviously a very serious and important event in the Round Table year.

"One thing, though," he went on. "We tend to get a bit under the weather at this do, you understand, but don't worry, we hire a minibus to get us there and back, so that there'll be no problems on the road."

With that, I went home, and Philippa seemed pleased that we were becoming a part of our community life.

On the appointed night, I dressed in my best bib and tucker, and gingerly navigated my way through the cement-mixers and all the paraphernalia of the building site to the end of the road, and waited for the minibus.

In due course, it arrived, and we were soon on our way to Alloway for this marvellous occasion.

I wanted to create a good impression right from the start, so I made sure that I was at the head of the queue for the drinks, so that I could order for our group.

"I'll have a pint of bitter, please," I said to the barman, "and what will everybody else have?"

There was a deathly hush from the men standing behind and around me. I could see the disapproving looks flitting from one face to another.

"What the hell have I done now?" I thought to myself, and then the penny dropped.

"No; I don't fancy beer tonight," I mumbled. "Shall we all have a wee dram?"

To a general chorus of approval and friendly banter, the atmosphere suddenly grew warm and hearty again, and I breathed a sigh of relief.

"Ay, laddie," grunted one enormously tall, bearded and kilted figure, obviously the type who would toss the caber half way round Alloway, "we all like a wee drram or two on this verrry special occasion."

The friend who had invited me in the first place turned to me and said, "Come with us, Keith; we all sit in small groups at the tables, and we usually get one or two drinks in, so that we don't have to keep going back to the bar. We share the costs, of course..."

"Of course," I chimed in, still eager to eliminate the recollection of my earlier gaff.

"That's great," he said, and he shouted across to the barman to put three bottles of whisky on the table. At that table, there were just six of us!

"Bloody hell!" I thought to myself. "What sort of a night is this going to be if these are just for starters!" We have Burns' Nights in Yorkshire, but nothing to compare with this.

Within a short space of time, the whisky stock began to diminish rapidly, and the volume of excited chatter increased as the atmosphere thawed.

Actors had been hired to declaim the poems of Burns, intoning them in fine Scottish accents. Then the Haggis was piped in in full solemnity, and the Ode and Grace repeated with great dignity and gravity. It was all very serious, but I was beginning to enjoy myself in this society.

The haggis was served. I'd not tasted haggis before but, after a few tentative mouthfuls, I began to enjoy its coarse, savoury taste.

"What do you think of this stuff?" asked a young chap, very quietly, sitting by me.

"I think it's great, wonderful!" I replied, enthusing strongly over this traditional fare. It must be good, if all these men wanted it. I wasn't going to be caught out again.

"He loves haggis," I heard him whisper to one or two of the others. Pairs of eyes opened wide, gazing across at me. I was the centre of admiration.

"We hate the stuff. Hold your plate up..." and the others started surreptitiously filling my plate with the portions they couldn't eat – even some from the other tables!

I finished up with a mound of haggis that got drier and drier with each mouthful, and soon I'd had more than I could comfortably manage. I felt that much of the haggis and myself would part company before the night's business was concluded, but honour now insisted I fulfil my role. The Tablers watched as I strove to diminish the heap, and I, conscious of their gaze, continued this task of Augean proportions. Eventually, each mouthful took on more and more the texture of a subtle blend of sawdust and grit.

I don't think I'll eat haggis ever again.

As the evening wore on, the Tablers became more and more inebriated. The first three bottles of whisky went, then another three, and, by this time, they didn't know whether it was Burns' Night or Pancake Tuesday. Nor me. I was in a dreadful state, and the room would not stay still.

Up to now, it had all been so serious. But, obviously, a significant moment in the celebration had arrived. One of the men produced, with studied care, a little black book from a small attaché case, and began to read.

I've never been so surprised in my life. This was the poetry of Burns that was never published – and almost every line and phrase made it abundantly clear just why. It was the most hair-curling stuff you're ever likely to meet outside a brown paper parcel. And all the Tablers sat there, laughing and joking, a jovially robust chorus, goaded on by the reader of the poems.

As far as I am able to recall, it must have been somewhere about 1 a.m. when we all staggered out into the cool freshness of the night air. After several hours in the heat of that room, the air hit us like a blanket.

We piled into the minibus, and, eventually, it came to a halt, and I found myself, I thought, standing by the roadside on the main road near our house. Another bloke had been thrown out at the same place, and in worse condition than myself

"Where do you live, laddie?" he managed to communicate.

I told him as best I could, my tongue and throat the consistency of old leather.

"I'll see you home, then," he slurred, and, grabbing me by the arm, he bundled me in the approximate direction of home. The journey was long and painful. We stumbled in the darkness over piles of bricks – there were no street lights as yet, of course – and collided with cement-mixers. There was mud everywhere, and much of it on us.

Philippa had stayed up for me and was watching from the dining-room window, and could just about make out the two shapes lurching up the road. I recall little from then on, till the following morning.

As it happened, a couple of weeks later, we were invited to a Round Table sherry morning, so I was able to renew acquaintance with one or two of those I had met on that unforgettable evening. Philippa and I were standing near a table, and a young man was sitting close by.

"Aren't you going to introduce me to your friend?" asked Philippa, nodding in the general direction of the young man. He looked equally mystified, never having laid eyes on me before. He smiled a sort of forced smile of recognition.

"Surely you haven't forgotten him already?" she continued, infuriatingly. "This is the young man who escorted you up our road on Burns' Night. Last time I saw you, you were climbing over a cement-mixer," she added.

The young man looked at me, and I looked at him. I could have sworn I'd never seen him before in my life.

"Oh, hallo. I'm very pleased to meet you," I said. In time, I got to know Dick Morton quite well.

If there is such a thing as a typical Scotsman, then Dick fitted that description absolutely.

I'd heard stories, also, about how mean some Scotsmen can be. I say 'some' Scotsmen, because the vast majority, I think, are as generous and liberal as anywhere in the world, and their hospitality is second to none.

Dick was a good bloke, but he was as mean and miserly as a latter day Scrooge.

One of his prized possessions was a labrador bitch of which he thought the world. By pure coincidence, Dick's next door neighbour owned a beautiful, pedigreed, prize-winning labrador dog.

"It's an awful lot of money," he said to me, very confidentially, one day, "to have the services of yon dog for my wee lass. I've a mind to make a hole in the fence and see if I can get the two together that way."

Sure enough, not long afterwards, the next door neighbour's dog found his way through the fence, and happened to encounter Dick's labrador, which was on heat. When it was discovered that Dick's labrador was pregnant, the neighbour was most apologetic.

"Oh, not to worry," said Dick. "I don't really want the pups, but we'll just have to manage."

And Dick ended up with a full litter of pedigree pups – just as he'd planned.

It took me a while to become adjusted to life in Scotland, and to get to know the problems of being in charge of a mill.

That first summer I was there, the weather was beautiful, and I remember one particular Sunday when everyone was sitting out in their gardens enjoying the summer warmth.

I, too, was taking a break.

Suddenly, the phone rang. It was the local police.

"Mr Haigh?"

"Yes," I said.

"Will you come down to the mill, please. All the doors are open and we were wondering if everything was alright."

I got into my car and hared off to the mill.

When I got there, the doors were wide open, and I could see straightaway that not only had two handcarts disappeared from the yard, but that half the bales of wool had gone! Half the mill's total stock of wool had been stolen!

One of the policemen asked me to go into the mill to see if anything was missing.

I said, "I don't need to go into the mill. I can see that half the entire stock's gone."

"Och," he said, "they're little beggars. You've got to watch 'em round here."

A masterly understatement.

It was clear what they'd done. They'd wheeled the bales away on the handcarts and wheeled them through the streets, past the gardens, with the people sitting there still enjoying the sunshine.

A couple of hours later, the police found the bales hidden in a ditch in a nearby wood.

And all these people must have watched the bales being wheeled past them, and never said a word. They knew who it was who'd done it too, but we could never find out. We got all the wool back, eventually, into the mill, but that was the sort of problem I began to meet in my first encounter as a mill manager. It was a pretty rough place, to say the least.

If that first summer encounter was not very promising, the first Christmas we were there promised even less.

Jim, as I have said, was a giant of a man, and a bully to boot. He wanted his own way, right or wrong, and he didn't care whose toes he trod on in the way.

Three weeks before Christmas, he called me into his office.

"Now then, Keith," he said, "I've decided that we're going to have a Christmas party."

"Sorry?"

I couldn't have heard him correctly.

"We're going to have a Christmas party – for the workers. We've got to get a good link between the employees and the management. OK? The only way I reckon we can do that is to have a Christmas party."

"Who had you thought of inviting?" I asked.

"All the bloody workers – who do you think?" He looked at me, as if I was barmy.

"Hang on a minute," I said. "Do you know what they're like when they've got a bit inside them?"

"If they work for us, they deserve a party. Just get one organised."

"Where had you thought of having this party?"

"I don't know. There must be plenty of places round about. Find one, then put up a notice and tell them they're coming to a party. We'll put it on for nothing. We'll give 'em a damn good night out."

"Oh, my godfathers!" I swore, under my breath.

The quality controller was a chap called John; he worked on the floor above, and I thought it might be an idea to get some help from him in this business.

"You won't believe this, John.   He wants us to organise a Christmas party for all the staff. Well, he asked me really, but I think you might like to come in on it."

"You must be joking!" he exclaimed. "What are we going to do?"

"Well, I don't know, but if he says we're having a Christmas party, I don't see how we can get out of it. We'll just have to get one organised."

That night, John and I set off into town to find a place where we could hold a party. One hotel had been highly recommended, and, when I spoke to the manager, he seemed very pleased to have us. It was quite a select place in its own gardens a little way off the main road – just the place for a quiet evening's drink for two. I dreaded to think what an invasion from our workers would do to it.

So, we booked the night, I arranged a bus to take us there, and then I put up a notice in the mill.

Within half a minute, all work had stopped, and the workers were crowding round this notice. It caused quite a stir, and within ten minutes every name was on the list!

There was no backing out now. I rang the bus company to order a bigger bus.

If I was apprehensive about the night before I'd made the arrangements, I was absolutely dreading it now. The possibilities of what could happen were too unpleasant to think of.

As the night of the party approached, my heart sank.

"We shan't get through the night," I said to Philippa. "You're going to have to help, and, whatever needs to be done, you'll have to lend a hand. John says he'll make sure that his wife will be there, and she'll help as well. They say they'll be going in their car, so that, if there is any trouble, they won't get involved.   At least they're coming," I said.

The day before the party was scheduled to take place, Jim, the managing director, came breezing into my office.

"Keith," he said, "I'm taking a holiday. I'm going to have a break."

"When are you going?" I enquired.

"I've decided that my wife and I are going tomorrow."

I couldn't believe it.

"Come on, Jim. We've the party tomorrow. Have you forgotten?"

"No, I haven't forgotten. You can cope."

What I thought at that moment is unprintable. "That's just the sort of thing you would do," I said to myself.

"I'll see you in the New Year. All the best."

And with that, he was gone.

Well, there was nothing now but to see this thing through.

The night finally arrived – the night I had been dreading, and nothing that I saw or heard made me pleased to change my mind. We all met at the mill, and all clambered on to the bus. I must admit I was surprised; I'd never seen some of these chaps all tidied up.

We got through the first course, then the second, and then on to dessert. So far, no trouble. My hopes were beginning to rise. But not for long. Catastrophe was just around the corner. I looked around. One or two were starting to talk quite loudly, and comments were being shouted down the table.

"And there's the dancing still to come," I thought. "What on earth's going to happen here?"

By 11.00 p.m., it began to get seriously out of hand. I could tell that by the way they started smashing up the bar.

"Come on, John. Let's get them into the bus as quick as we can, one way or another."

John found the bus driver.

"My mate's inside. He'll get them out to you," said John. "Would you make sure they don't get off again?"

The driver agreed to stand guard by the door, and see that they didn't get off again.

For the next twenty minutes or so – it seemed much longer! – I propelled these drunken men out towards the bus, till the last one had gone. I mumbled something to the manager about the mill paying for the damages, and beat a hasty retreat.

When I reached the bus, I was about to breathe a sigh of relief, but was horrified to see the bus driver guarding what was nearly an empty bus! A number of them had found the back door, forced it open, and were now back in the hotel via a back door! My worst nightmares were coming truer by the minute. The whole farcical scene would have been comical, if I hadn't been responsible – and angry.

It took us nearly another hour to prise them out of the bar, by which time most of the men were fully committed to whatever state alcohol reduces them – some quarrelsome, some shouting incoherently, some singing unmelodiously, some in a state of maudlin sentimentality, and some already in blissful unconsciousness, snoring loudly. We finally got them on to the bus, all locked in.

I shouted to the bus driver, "On your way, mate!" and he sped off up the road and disappeared from sight.

"Thank heaven for that," I said, and the four of us – Philippa, John and his wife, and myself – all breathed a sigh of relief. I wouldn't have been the bus driver for all the tea in China. I'll never know how he managed to cope with that heaving – and I mean heaving – drunken mass of humanity on their way home. But rather him than me.

So, we stood there outside the hotel. I said, "Well, that's it, then. How do you fancy going in for a drink to relax before we go home?" They readily agreed.

We went in. The manager was looking less than pleased. A waitress came over to us.

"At least it's all very quiet now," I said, trying my best to put things right.

"Well, that depends," she said. "What're you going to do about your mate in the back room?"

"Pardon?"

"Your friend, in the back room – what are you going to do about him?"

"They've all gone home in the bus."

"All bar one," she said. "There's one laid on the floor. I want him out of the place."

We all trooped into the back room, and there was this big fellow, whom I recognised as the foreman of the yarn-packing department, lying on the floor, spark out. Andrew Jamieson was a chap who never ever missed work. He was a surly, sullen man, always frowning, never smiled, never spoke unless he had to, and even then wouldn't utter two words if one would do. On his way into the mill, you'd say, "Mornin', Andrew," and all you'd get would be a cross between a cough and a snarl for reply. He was an odd fellow, but a tremendous worker, and massive with it.

We walked into this back room, and there he was lying on the rug in front of the fire.

"Why on earth...? We ought to have had him on the bus with the others."

"I couldna move him," the waitress snapped. "You'll have tae tak him hame."

I asked John if he knew where this Andrew lived, but he had no idea. After a struggle, we managed to get him on to the back seat of the car, and we set off.

We'd not the foggiest idea where he lived, and so we went round and round the centre of the town, hoping we should meet someone who might know where he lived. I didn't fancy the alternative of opening up the mill, getting into the office to find his file and his address.

Eventually, we saw a policeman and stopped the car. "We've got a fellow in the back here. He's a little the worse for drink, but we don't know where he lives."

The policeman took a look at him, and smiled.

"Oh, I know him," he said. "If his wife sees him in this condition, she'll knock seven bells out of him."

There was something slightly humorous in this. He was well over six feet tall, and must have weighed nearly sixteen stone.

The policeman helped us find the house. It was a little terrace house with a garden on to the road.

We frogmarched this huge hulk up the path, and rested him gently against the front door. Very gracefully, he slid down the door, and came to rest sitting over the threshold. I knocked gently on the door.

The house had been in darkness, but now a light came on, as we made our way back to the car – we thought she wouldn't wish to speak to us so late at night.

As his wife opened the door, he fell backwards into the hall on to a slippy mat that was sufficient to cause him to slide along it. Our final recollection of this scene was of his wife soundly slapping him before slamming shut the door. It was a fitting end to a nightmare evening.

Next morning was Saturday morning, and we usually worked up to lunchtime.

82

"Well," I said to John. "That'll be it. We shan't see Andrew today."

"Don't you worry," he replied. "He'll be there."

We walked down into the mill and across to the yarn-packing department.

There was Andrew, his head down, working away - and not a glimmer of a word to say about the previous night's adventure - as if nothing had happened – but, judging by what we had seen just before the front door had closed the previous evening, I bet she'd knocked the traditional seven bells out of him! What sort of a night he'd had, goodness only knows.

I hope no one ever asks me to organise another Christmas party, although, funnily enough, quite a number of the blokes made it known to me that they were pleased they'd gone, and that they'd had a great time – if only they could remember what had happened!

In the first summer after I'd joined Round Table, I also came to know the chap who owned the local garage, and his pal. They had a motor boat near Troon, and, one day, I received a phone call at the mill, inviting me to join them for an evening.

"We're just going for a trip up the coast as far as Cumbrae, and we'll stop there and have a few wee drams."

The idea sounded good to me, and so I asked Philippa if she minded my going out that evening, as I had been invited along with these two friends. Philippa didn't mind.

So they picked me up and off we went down to their motor boat. Just about a mile off the mainland coast is the island of Great Cumbrae. It was a beautiful evening, and the journey was smooth and pleasant. The boat was fast enough to be exhilarating, without being too fast for comfort. It was good to be there, speeding up the coast, with such an impressive backdrop as Ailsa Craig.

It didn't take us long to reach our destination, moor the boat, and find our way to the local hostelry.

An island like Cumbrae was, of course, a law unto itself. I'm not sure if it is, these days. For instance, 'closing time' is when you've had enough, not some arbitrary, fixed and unwelcome conclusion.

Consequently, we finished up well into the night. It was pitch black when we finally prised ourselves from the pub, and it took us a while to locate where we'd moored the boat.

We clambered unsteadily aboard, and then one of my colleagues said, "We like skiing in the dark. We do a bit of water skiing; it's good fun."

"You're joking," I said, but, illustrating they were not joking, both my colleagues were by now busy donning rubber suits and helmets and goggles and snorkels and skis and whatever.

I couldn't believe it – and especially in their condition. They must have been mad.

"You know how to drive the boat?" one of them asked. "Just keep going, and we'll follow."

And with the absolute minimum of instruction, and even less of an idea where exactly to head the boat, we set off, negotiated our way gingerly out of the harbour, and set course for the mainland. There was a complete learner-driver at the wheel, and two sozzled skiers trailing behind.

How we ever got back, heaven only knows. They kept falling off into the black waters; they'd shout, I'd bring the boat to a halt somehow, they'd shout "OK", then off we'd go again, heading to where we thought the mainland was.

It seems unbelievable now, but that was exactly how it happened, and I suppose it was more by a great deal of good fortune, than anything else that, firstly, nothing seriously went wrong, and, secondly, we were able to moor the boat at the same spot from which we'd set out some unsuspecting hours before.

I shudder, now, to think of the attendant dangers to which we had all been exposed, and the sheer fun of it recedes slightly into the background. Of course, Philippa never knew – not, at least until some years had passed between the event and the telling of it, and when it didn't really make any difference. But, what a night!

CHAPTER 5

Three years passed very quickly, three happy years for the family and myself, and, if the business had continued to flourish, I might have still been there. But there came a day when I realised that the mill was not making the progress that it should have been making. It was clear that Jim, the managing director, was having trouble with the owners of the mill and was thinking of leaving. It was just as clear that, without Jim, the mill was unlikely to continue to prosper.

I decided that, if Jim was going, then so was I – there was no future for me there if Jim was not in control. He'd been an odd chap to work for but by and large, we'd got on well together, and we'd built the business up. It was time to be on the move again.

In the late sixties and early seventies, if you had qualifications, and you weren't greedy for money, there were plenty of jobs available in the textile industry. I was fortunate that a vacancy arose at a mill in Farndale, and, almost before I knew it, I was on my way back to the West Riding. Scotland had been good, but I wasn't sorry to be back in Yorkshire, though there were many good friends I was leaving behind.

Arkwright's was a very old established firm, making superb quality cloths. They had made their reputation on producing very good cloths for uniforms, and supplied most of the regiments of the British Army. It was a very interesting place to come into – not much money, but plenty of enjoyment, and the start of eight happy years with the firm.

At Arkwright's, tradition was everything, including the method of using teasels to raise the nap on cloth. It was a mill where the wools were selected with infinite care – even down to choosing the wool from specific farms in Australia, because they provided just the kind of wool that was required. For me, it was like an Aladdin's cave, with wool the treasure.

In this new environment, I felt instantly at home. But I'm a great believer in treating people the way you hope they would treat you, and one of the first things that cropped up at Arkwright's was dealing with a face from the past.

In fact, it was going back to the time when I had given my notice in at Fratton's some ten years before I came to Arkwright's.

The mill manager there had been John Sykes. He'd been very surly with me when I'd told him I was leaving – I'd just been offered the job in Ireland. (If only I'd known then what I know now!) I remember him telling me, very belligerently, that I'd have to work a month's notice, and only get paid for two of the four weeks.

"I'm not having that," I said. "That's not right."

"Those are the rules round here, lad, whether you like it or not. You'd better stick by them."

I decided not to make a scene; I'd work two weeks, and then tackle him again.

For the next two weeks we kept apart from each other, but I was still just as determined he wasn't going to get away with what was obviously unjust and unfair.

After two weeks, I picked up my wage, and went in to see him again. As I walked in, he looked at me, then turned away, as if he were busy with something. Already I could feel myself becoming angry at this show of ignorance.

"I've worked two weeks," I said, "and I'm prepared to work the other two – but I want paying for them. I think that's only fair, Mr Sykes."

He turned, and looked at me for a moment, almost in surprise. Then he started waving the papers he was holding in front of my face.

"You've got all the bloody money you're going to get off this firm!" he shouted.

"Right, then. I want my cards. I'm going."

I'll never forget that moment. He came close to me and looked me straight in the eyes.

"You think you're very good, don't you. But I can wield a lot of influence, and if you think you can go out of here without working these next two weeks, I'll mark your cards for the rest of your career. You'll never get on anywhere. I'll see to that."

I remember thinking what a rotten thing to say. But I wasn't intimidated by it.

"Just give me my cards."

I stood my ground, and he backed away. He didn't say another word.

And that was it; I just walked out. There haven't been many occasions when I've felt myself to be in a corner – thankfully – but this was one time I knew I was doing what I thought was right.

Well, that was about ten years before I took the job at Arkwright's, and there I was, nearly a decade on, sitting in my office, the first morning.

The telephone rang. It was Peter Arkwright.

"There's a chap waiting in reception. Perhaps you'd like to go and have a word with him; the sooner you get to meet these wool men, the better. See what he's got to offer. If he's got anything worthwhile, we'll have a look at it."

So I went down to reception.

There, sitting in a corner, waiting to see the wool buyer was my old boss from Fratton's, John Sykes. To say he was surprised is an understatement; but I was no less taken by surprise myself. He took one look at me.

"Keith!" he blurted out. "What the hell are you doing here?"

"I'm the new wool buyer. What can I do for you?"

He stood there, collecting his thoughts, all the time looking extremely embarrassed. He hadn't forgotten what he'd said to me all those years ago – and I'd certainly not forgotten. For a moment there was an awkward silence. We didn't need to exchange any words.

Finally, he stepped forward, shook me by the hand, and muttered, "I wish you all the best, lad," and walked out without a backward glance.

I didn't make him go; he just left of his own accord – not that I bore him any ill will after all that time. But he knew that there could be no business between us, conducted, as deals always used to be, as a matter of trust and mutual respect.

I never came across him again. But it taught me a lesson not to make threats that might, one day, come back to you, as his threats had done, nor to let the mouth rule the head.

Now, when I joined Arkwright's in the early seventies, as I said, the firm enjoyed a considerable reputation for making uniform cloths. In the entrance lobby was a display showing the uniforms of all the British Regiments, and the uniforms that Arkwright's had made for them.

"We've got a funny enquiry this morning," said Peter, one morning. He had just been opening the post.

"What's that?" I asked.

"Ministry of Defence – asking us for some khaki cap cloth. Ee, I've not seen an order for this before." (He knew the stock from top to bottom.)

"It's a funny one, is this. It's got me flummoxed." The enquiry had a reference number on it.

"Come on," he said. "We'll go and see if we can find this reference number."

Peter took me into a room I'd not yet discovered, having only just started working there. Within, the room was a big, dark, dusty office, with a high ceiling – so high it seemed to have receded into nothing, hidden by a cloud of dust.

He switched on the light; a bulb cast a feeble glow round about, shedding a wan light on rows and rows of boxes piled high; they, too, disappeared into the gloom above.

He tugged a pair of solid, wooden stepladders into place against one side, and turned to me and said, "You go up there. You'll find a box with this reference number on."

Standing on the top of these steps, I started blowing dust off these rows of old boxes, revealing, as I did so, labels in beautiful copperplate handwriting, and all the boxes were in numerical order. It was easy to find the box with our reference on it – right at the top, thick in dust.

"Have you found it?" he shouted up.

'I've got this…"

"Fetch it down, then. Let's have a look."

I came down the stepladders and handed him the box. He blew the rest of the dust away.

"By, that's it! I've never gone back so far before."

We opened up the mahogany box, and, inside, was a scrap of khaki cap cloth, a reference number, and the year 1912 on a piece of paper.

"Good Lord!" exclaimed Peter. "That's my grandfather's handwriting, is that!"

Somebody in the Ministry of Defence had ordered this cap cloth in 1912 for a particular Regiment, and had made a mistake. Instead of ordering a roll or ten rolls, they'd put another nought on! We'd one hundred rolls of cap cloth!

You can imagine how long that must have lasted. And here we were, in 1970, and suddenly they'd run out of cap cloth at the

Ministry. They must have looked back through their records and found out that it was Arkwright's who had made this cap cloth all those years before.

"Well," said Peter, still looking in astonishment at the order. "We don't really want it, do we? We'll have to... I don't even know how to make it."

He looked puzzled, as he peered into the box. Inside the box was a little blend sheet, with all the details of how it had been made. Incredible!

"By hell!" exclaimed Peter. " If we could buy some wool like this..."

The reference numbers were years out of date, old numbers of firms that had long since disappeared, wool merchants who had gone out of business many years before.

I couldn't help thinking, "Who was the person, who was it, sitting in some little Government office down in London, who had unearthed Arkwright's name and the reference number for this khaki cap cloth? Did he really think the world had stood still for eighty years? That things hadn't changed? When he made out the order, did he really expect that someone would have the cloth there, just ready and waiting?" Surely, it must have been a triumph for hope over expectation.

But tradition was tradition, and, if tradition decreed that Arkwright's had provided the cloth in the past, then Arkwright's must provide the cloth today. That was how the system worked, and that was how they wanted it.

"I tell you what," said Peter, "to make sure we don't get the order, we'll overprice it – cost it out and multiply it by four or five times; they won't want to know, then. There's no way we can do this cloth."

We costed out the order.

Less than two weeks after we'd sent in our estimated costs multiplied several times over – back came the reply. The MoD required two rolls of cap cloth! Isn't that wonderful! When times are hard, you chase around for any orders you can land; when you don't want them, they come in anyway!

I think, in this instance, we could have charged just what we wanted. Tradition demanded it should be our cloth, no matter what the price.

I suppose, in the end, they knew what they were doing – they got their cap cloth – and a good blend it was, as well. But those days have long since gone – and more's the pity.

In the seventies, if tradition persisted in little Government offices in London, there was still an equally strong emphasis on tradition in the mills and factories in the north.

With tradition went secrecy; each mill jealously guarded its methods and products. Nobody had to find out what the mill down the road was making; every other mill was on its own tack, trying to keep its own secrets to itself. It became a battle of wits, a cat and mouse game, from mill to mill, to stay ahead of the opposition.

The tradition at Arkwright's went back to the very beginning of the Australian wool trade, and the very first clip of wool that came from Botany Bay was actually transported to Arkwright's, and was made into cloth there – the first bale of Australian wool.

That bale was sent across by one of Mr Arkwright's ancestors, who was a vicar out in Australia. That's how far back tradition went at Arkwright's, and that was why it played such an important part in establishing a reputation in the textile world second to none.

Maybe tradition was the death of it; it wouldn't be like that today – it's all about costs and outputs nowadays, not who can produce the best.

The mill owner's house used to be situated in the park at the side of the mill, and, in those days, the responsibility for buying in the wool at the London wool sales rested with the mill owner himself.

On wool-buying mornings, once a month, the office staff would look out of their window overlooking the entrance to the mill; in time they would see the boss coming out of his house about 8.30, his morning paper neatly tucked under his arm.

They'd watch him get to the little gate at the bottom of his drive; they'd see him turn down the bit of road which led into the mill yard. They'd all sit there and take bets on whether he'd turn right to the station to catch the train to London, to go to the wool sales, or turn left to come into the mill. His decision would depend on the sales report in the newspaper, which he read over the breakfast table, and on which wools were up for sale and worth buying.

In the 1970s, all the wool was bought in London, at the wool auctions, but, now, all the colonial wool sales are held in Bradford. It was during my time at Arkwright's that the change to Bradford was made. Though economically it made sense for the wool sales to be transferred to Bradford, it marked the end of an era for the northern wool-buyers, who used to go to London each month and who regarded the day as one of the high spots of the month – it was a good day out and was treated as quite an event by the mill owners.

Mr Arkwright used to meet another mill owner from a nearby mill, and together they would make the journey down to the sales in London. They'd catch the train to King's Cross, take a taxi to the Wool Exchange, make their purchases, return by taxi to King's Cross, and take the train back north.

And this had been their routine, month in, month out, year in, year out, for many years.

As the day for the transfer to the north grew near, and they realised that they would no longer be making this monthly journey south, it dawned on them that they had been going to London all these years, but had never actually seen the place!

"Fred," said my boss, "when the sales are over today, let's go and have a look round London, and see what it's all about, shall we?"

Fred readily agreed to this suggestion.

So when the sales were over – about 3.00 p.m. – they hailed a taxi, and asked the driver to take them to St Paul's.

They duly arrived outside the magnificent building, and could not fail to be impressed.

"That's a grand-looking place," said Peter Arkwright. "Let's take a look inside."

They moved slowly along, taking in as much as they could, until they were standing beneath the majestic dome of the cathedral.

"Now then, Fred, what's tha think o' that, then? It's bloody real, in't it?"

"By shots!" says Fred. "I've never seen owt like it in my life. It's bloody marvellous. Just look at the size of it!"

He craned his neck to take in the full glory of the dome.

"How many hundred bales of wool do you reckon we could store in this place?"

For Fred, beauty was synonymous with storage capacity, in this instance, and the potential he imagined for St Paul's was strictly utilitarian. Not all mill owners, however, were so single-minded – which is just as well!

The dawn of enlightenment comes more slowly to some than to others, and practical considerations often far outweigh other factors. Utility and art are rarely good bedfellows, it seems. The change to Bradford for the wool sales was, culturally, a backward step for the mill owners and managers of the north. In time, they might have found that London had more to offer than wool sales. On the other hand, being typical of many northerners, they might not have bothered to find out.

CHAPTER 6

Whilst I was at Arkwright's, I was re-introduced to the world of Round Table – that national organisation of young professional and businessmen, charity fund-raisers, do-gooders in the community, and men whose prime ambition is to have a good time together. I'd enjoyed my time with the 'Tablers' in Scotland, and I was happy to take up this part of social living again.

Up and down the country, members of these clubs meet in back rooms of pubs or social centres to discuss, over a meal and a pint, what they can do to help the community, and how to enjoy themselves doing it.

When I joined, I was at that sort of age when things like having good friends, and meeting new people, and enjoying myself, took on a significantly more serious role in my life, and not just in my life, but in Philippa's life, too. The reason was not hard to find. We couldn't have foreseen then the momentous changes which were to befall our lives, coming to us so completely unexpectedly.

On a gloriously sunny day in July, Philippa gave birth to our first son, a brother to Joanne. His birth was complicated, but, tiny though he was, our new arrival could not have been more welcome. We loved him from the start, and prayed that all would be well with him.

His first weeks were spent in an incubator, as he fought to survive, and twice a day we'd go to the hospital to see him. Each day we'd notice the changes in him, and thrill to the anticipation of the day we could bring him home.

It was a battle he won, in time, and the day came when we were allowed to take this little bundle home with us, and, oh, what a day that was. Royalty couldn't have received a warmer welcome. Fewer joys are more satisfying than having a new-born baby in the house, and John, as we had decided to call him, had made our family life complete.

The first inkling we had that all was not well came out of the blue – a message that the hospital wished to see John again, as soon as possible.

It was with a sense of foreboding that we returned to the same hospital we had so recently left in joy. This time our mood was sombre; we knew, or felt we knew, something must be wrong. We were soon to find out.

Tests confirmed what the doctors had suspected; we sat in an office, with John lying on a bed in the room close by, and a doctor calmly informing us that we had a Down's syndrome baby – a Mongol child – that we should think about placing him in a home, and forget about him.

"The best thing you can do is to start thinking about having another child," the doctor said, brusquely, and, with that pronouncement, he left us. We sat there, looking at each other, absolutely stunned. There was nothing to add, and we felt, suddenly, the weight of a new and terrible burden. Philippa cried, as I have never seen her cry before; it was a bleak and desperately sad moment in our lives.

Left to ourselves, we dressed John, and took him home with us.

In the car, we couldn't speak, and the journey passed in silence, as we strove to come to terms with what we now knew. It was a very different future we could see in front of us; we knew that things would never be quite the same again.

The days and weeks that followed were, indeed, difficult for us. I, at least, could throw myself into my work with sufficient zeal and dedication to put thoughts of family aside for each working day. Philippa lived with the situation each day, and couldn't escape. She couldn't bear the thought, even, of taking John for a walk in his pram anywhere near the Special school in the village where we lived. She had a hard time of it in those early days.

In short, we lived through the next few months in a state of shock. I could see each day the stress that Philippa endured. There was one thing on which Philippa and I agreed without reservation: this child of ours was not going to be put away in some home, to be brought up by people we didn't know – or didn't care for him, the way we would care for him. It became a source of strength that we would win through in our own way. He was ours, we would love him, and we would give him more love than any other child could ever have had. And Joanne, too, became the most loving older sister any boy could wish to have. The family bond grew strong. But nothing came easily for us in those days, and I remember we came to know our physical, emotional and psychological limitations like days of the week.

It is not necessary to dwell on this aspect of our domestic life, nor to speak of the years of close attention and patient care, and the endless times when energy was sapped, exhaustion played havoc with sleep, and tempers flared through sheer exasperation, as John demanded our time and supervision.

Time, however, changes all things; nothing lasts, good or bad.

His boyhood was a mixture of fun and fear, as we groped our way through each new difficulty.

His youth was, every day, another voyage in uncharted territory for us, but friends and relatives rallied round, and helped provide the support and company he needed. We couldn't have asked for more.

His manhood was sheer pleasure, as he learned to exert more independence, develop his own interests, attend college and make new friends for himself. Each day we were rewarded for ignoring the hospital doctor's advice of putting him in a home. The only home he knew was ours.

When I look back to those days, and when I see now, in retrospect, the future that we imagined then, I can afford to smile, for out of our seeming tragedy came love, and joy, and years of happiness. John grew up strong and healthy. He coped with language, learned to express himself for all needful occasions, and was full of love and laughter – and, indeed, still is, to this day. He has repaid, thousands of times over, the love we gave him in his struggling infancy and childhood.

Against this background of uncertainties at home, my work provided a refuge and a source of satisfaction. Arkwright's was a good place to be in the 1970s.

I also felt – now that I was back in Yorkshire – that I wanted to make some sort of contribution to the community in which I was living, and help those less favoured than myself. Whether this urge was triggered by having John at home or not, I don't know. Suffice to say, the company and activities of the men in the local Round Table club supplied a need I felt at that time. They were a good bunch of men, and, during my time with them, we had – Philippa, of course, was invited to all the social occasions – many happy hours in their company.

The club organised a number of events for charity, and we raised quite a lot of money for deserving causes. Being still youngish, energetic and enthusiastic, we indulged in various odd schemes in the name of making money for charity.

For some reason, unknown to me at the time, it fell to my lot one year to be responsible for organising the traditional 'Stag Night', not just for our club but for a number of clubs in the district. Feminists may wince, but the central ingredient of all Round Table Stag Nights was the appearance and performance of strippers.

It had been traditional also that this event would normally take place at the local Territorial Army barracks in the sergeants' mess. I soon got the hang of what was needed to make the arrangements – the venue was confirmed, the Round Table clubs informed, and, most importantly, the strippers booked. There didn't seem to be any particular difficulty in organising an event such as this, but how wrong could I be!

I got home from work the day before the event to be informed that there had been a telephone call from the Sergeant at the sergeants' mess, very urgent, to ring him back. I rang him straightaway.

"What's up, Bill?"

"Ah, Keith, glad you could ring. I'm sorry, I'm afraid you're going to have to cancel the 'do' for tomorrow. I've just had a phone call to tell me that there'll be an Area Office Inspection tomorrow night. There'll be all the top brass and their wives here. If they find out that there are strippers on the premises, they'll court-martial me on the spot."

He sounded very agitated.

"We can't have you-know-what going on at the same time they're here. Sorry, Keith, to let you down at such short notice."

That was a real bombshell. I was in a pickle.

"Well, Bill, there's no way I can contact all the chaps coming tomorrow. They've all been told about it, and they're coming from all over the region. It's got to go on tomorrow. Anyway, if I cancel it now, we'll lose all the money we were needing to raise for this year's charity – and, besides, they'll lynch me."

"Well, I don't know what we can do..."

I thought for a while.

"Look, Bill, leave it with me. I'll sort something out." (Why I say things like that when I haven't the faintest notion what to do puzzles me.)

"How the hell can you do that?"

"Just leave it to me," I said.

Anything would be better than incurring the wrath of a couple of hundred men.

A sleepless and restless night followed. But by the following morning, I thought I'd got the inklings of a plan.

That evening, there were upwards of two hundred men waiting to see a show. There was a comedian and there were four women.

The Sergeant was there, too; his face was a lighter shade of flour.

"Don't worry!" I said to him, with more conviction in my voice than I actually felt. "We've got it sorted out."

He looked less than reassured.

We put the girls in a room, telling them not to come out until they received word. We told the comedian – Sam Baldwin – to get himself out to the front, and to tell jokes – clean ones only for as long as he could.

"I don't know any clean ones!" he exclaimed in horror.

"Just do your best," we said.

Having explained to all the men in the audience the reason for this charade, they threw themselves into the spirit of it with considerable enthusiasm.

An assorted audience of men all sat there and listened to Sam for what seemed an eternity, and laughed and clapped and cheered loudly and raucously the feeblest of jokes.

Sam, of course, very quickly ran out of clean jokes, and had to be prompted from the floor with some of the most puerile jokes that any of the Tablers and their friends could come up with. The pints of beer in their hands emptied at regular intervals, and, no doubt, the alcohol added its own zest to the proceedings.

Every now and again, VIP's would put their heads round the door, see all the men laughing and enjoying themselves in harmless fun, and would then withdraw. But the strain was beginning to tell on Sam, and he was becoming increasingly tongue-tied, wondering what more he could tell us.

Just when despair was setting in, one of the VIP officers came in and said, "We're leaving now, gentlemen. Enjoy the rest of your evening. Carry on."

And they did!

The Sergeant was still beside himself with anxiety, and kept murmuring to himself, "Never again, never again," as he stood there, shaking his head slowly from side to side.

Eventually, the first of the girls was ready to begin. The lights were dimmed, and the throbbing music began to pulse through the floorboards.

As she came on to the 'floor' – a space barely larger than an average lounge – the men drew closer, crowding round, like bees round a honey pot. Social historians would have a field day, accounting for this behaviour, and, in truth, not a very savoury spectacle.

The M.C. announced each of the girls, every now and again his microphone emitting a high-pitched whine, as he strayed out of line. Exotic names, like Samantha, Cheryl, Melanie and Davina served to raise the girls' status on to a higher plane, and their costumes attempted to reinforce this degree of sophistication.

With the aid of a chair, each stripper, in turn, would perform her unsubtle act against a background of 'mood' music, on the one hand, and sporadic cheers that signalled the removal of each garment, on the other. Each garment was then nonchalantly draped over the chair, and, when all was over, summarily and unceremoniously gathered up, as the girl would run for the sanctuary of a door at the back of the space where she had performed.

At least, none of the girls made any pretentious claims that what she was doing should be viewed as 'art'.

Though the purpose of the girls was basically the same, only the mode of arriving at that point, and the length of time taken to do so, differed in any measure.

Perhaps, too, the degree of sensuality of each girl's act might be taken into account, as one or two of these particular girls were obviously more concerned, during their performance, with what shopping needed to be done the following day. Once or twice, some of the men in the audience reminded them what they were there for.

If the suspense became too much, there'd be cries of, "Get on with it!" followed by more cheers.

Each act was roundly cheered and clapped and whistled by the assembled host of men, as she took her bow, when the music juddered to a climactic halt. A pose would be struck, but the mask was off, and the tawdry reality was apparent to all. No one seemed to care; the taped music was already beginning to herald the start of the next act, giving the men just enough time to replenish their drinks at the bar.

Readers may draw their own conclusions about this spectacle, and may seriously wish to question why two hundred or more business and professional men find pleasure in attending such an event. Perhaps the men's desire to raise money for needy charities outweighed any moral scruples they may have entertained. There again, pigs might fly.

Before very long, the show was over, the lights came on again, and the M.C. thanked everybody for coming, telling the men how much they appreciated their support, and how much money had been made for charity. It was, everyone agreed, a good night.

Perhaps the Sergeant was one of the few to raise a dissenting voice. He was adamant that that was it, as far as he was concerned, and he declared he would never be party to another such evening.

The role of Pandar never again sat on his shoulders.

Almost a year to the day later, I knew what that Sergeant meant only too well, and understood exactly the anxiety he had felt the previous year. I should have learned from him. I wonder, sometimes, whether we ever learn anything from our experiences; they don't seem to have any appreciable effect upon our actions – merely enabling us to recognise we've been in a particular situation before. Which may, or may not, help!

I suppose it was my misfortune to have to organise the event again – the Tablers were relying on me to come up with a new venue, now that the barracks were no longer available.

The only reason I can come up with for me to have been organising an evening like this is that I've always found it easier to say 'yes' to people rather than 'no' – and that has been the simple cause of my undoing on a number of occasions! A pretty feeble explanation, I admit, but the best I can come up with at the moment.

It occurred to me that, with some adaptation, the canteen at the mill would be a most suitable venue for hosting the event.

After checking that the canteen would suffice admirably, and that I could obtain a key to the mill to let us in and out, and that we could run our own bar, everything progressed fine – fine, that is, until the afternoon preceding the Stag Night.

"I hear you're holding a little party for some of your friends from the Round Table," said Mrs Arkwright, the wife of the owner of the mill. She was what can only be termed a 'nice' person – no airs and graces, nothing silly about her, just a very nice, pleasant person to know. In the mill she liked to make herself known, and she kept a motherly eye on the staff.

"That's right, Mrs Arkwright. We usually get together each year to have a social evening."

"Lovely!" she exclaimed. "And you do so much good for charity, I understand."

"That's quite correct. Any money we raise goes straight to charity."

"How splendid!" she said. "As you have been unable to use the canteen for catering for your friends, some of the ladies from the office and myself have decided that we shall pop in to make you and your friends just a little buffet supper, just to help your evening along. Just a few sandwiches and sausage rolls – that sort of thing."

I looked carefully at her; she was not joking.

"Er..er..." My god! I was lost for words. I couldn't exactly say, "Sorry, Mrs Arkwright, we've got two hundred young men coming here tonight to watch four strippers perform..." Somehow I don't think she would have approved.

"Well, that's very good of you, Mrs Arkwright, but I don't think there's any need for you to put yourself to that trouble. We're quite..."

"Nonsense! The ladies and I will be delighted to be there to help." And off she went.

I thought, "What am I going to do? This is worse than last year. How can I get out of this one?"

A bold approach was called for. Later in the afternoon I went to see her.

"Look, Mrs Arkwright, we very much appreciate your kindness, but, you know, it's a man's evening, and one or two of the men might start telling jokes that might be a little... er... risqué, for the ladies. I would hate the ladies to hear..."

"I gather you'd rather we were not there this evening, Mr Haigh?"

"I think, perhaps, it would be better if you were not – just in case," I said, seriously.

"And you are sure you would not want me to come in on my own to make some sandwiches, then?"

"Thank you, Mrs Arkwright, but I'm absolutely certain."

"Oh, well, if you think not..."

But when it came to the evening itself, and the 'show' was in full swing – in more senses than one! – I died a thousand deaths, fearing every moment to see Mrs Arkwright appearing at the door. I spent the whole evening going up and down the corridors, checking that she was not coming in to make sandwiches, in spite of what was said.

If only she'd known, there'd have been more than a few raised eyebrows – and, yet, I have a vague suspicion that she knew all along what we were up to, and was probably, even at the moment of my tramping the corridors, sitting at home with an occasional smile on her lips.

Like the Sergeant the previous year, I didn't think my nerves would stand another such evening. "Never again, never again," I echoed the Sergeant, and that was the last of the Stag Nights that I had anything to do with.

One of the traditions of Arkwright's was the making of cloths for uniforms for the naval cadets at Dartmouth. This uniform cloth was made from pure indigo dye. What used to happen there – tradition being as it was – was that the wool was dyed in exactly the same way as it had been for generations, a pure indigo dyestuff.

We used to send the wool away to a little dyehouse in Dewsfield, and it used to come back dyed indigo blue. And it was the most horrible wool you've ever seen, because, when it came back, the dye was never very fast, and it used to come off in hazy blue clouds.

The poor devils who had to blend the stuff used to get blue in their hair, under their nails, in their ears - anywhere the dye could find a spot to land. But the method that was used was the traditional method, and everybody had to put up with it. If it was tradition, you had to do it.

For years it had simply been a question, when an order came in for blue-dyed cloth, for me to get some wool out of the warehouse, and send a lorry over to Frith's – and the wool would come back dyed indigo blue. That is, until one day we received a letter from Frith's, informing us that, after one hundred years of dyeing wool indigo, they had decided to cease their services. "Consequently, we will be unable to dye any more of your wool."

When the boss read this letter, he nearly blew a fuse.

"Frith's aren't carrying on. They're finishing," he muttered. "What the heck are we going to do? We'd better try and sort something out pretty quickly."

He went away, still clutching the letter. In two minutes he was back.

"I tell you what, Keith. We'll buy the dyehouse. We've got to keep to the same method; everything's got to be dyed the same way, it's always been done like this. We can't start changing tradition."

I was in charge of the wool-dyeing process at the time. He said to me, "Get yourself over to the dyehouse, and see what it's like. Let's know what's needed and we'll bring the machinery over here, and we'll dye the wool here."

Within the next couple of days, I'd fixed up to go across to speak to the manager of the dyehouse. This dyehouse was situated down a small back street, about a quarter of a mile from our mill, not far from the centre of the town. It all had that 'run-down' feel about it; it had seen better days.

I went to the office and said that I had an appointment to see the manager to discuss the dyehouse.

"Eh, by gum, lad, tha wants ta buy it, dus' tha?" (He couldn't have sounded more Yorkshire if he'd tried. So broad was his accent, he was almost a caricature, a southerner's idea of the typical Yorkshireman. All he needed were the flat cap and braces to complete the image.)

This was Lewis Frith, the manager of this long-established dyeworks. He was a blunt, straight-speaking Yorkshireman, dark-haired, going grey, with a faint touch of blue round the hairline. Honest as the day is long; if I'm not taking the allusion too far, he was a real dyed-in-the-wool character!

"We may be interested in purchasing your indigo dyeing machinery," I replied, "but we don't really know the in's and out's of..." I tried to appear businesslike and formal. He put his hand on my forearm - funny how some people do this.

"Don't worry," he said, as if confidentially. "I'll show thi 'ow it wuks."

Fred Trueman couldn't have said it better.

We made our way down some stone steps and in through a dark passage into the dye room.

"I'll give ya't recipes, and ya just put stuff in one end, and it cums out o' t'other. The's nowt to it."

"That's good," I said. "We'd like to dismantle it and take it up to Arkwright's. We'll put it in up there – and carry on with the tradition."

"Reet, lad, let's have a look at it."

As I stepped into the dye room, and my eyes became accustomed to the dim light inside, I could hardly believe what I saw.

Inside the room was a machine that had been new when spinning was in its infancy, and the whole room was a mass of blue. There was blue on the ceiling, blue on the floor, blue on the walls and in the middle of this dingy blue mess was the oldest blue machine imaginable, just a throbbing mass of tubes, belts, cogs and gears, covered in blue.

Lewis looked at the machine for a moment, then looked at me, pride in his eye, "It's real, in't it! In't it just great!"

"It's absolutely unbelievable, Mr Frith," I replied. "My god, how does it work?"

"As I say, the's nowt to it. You switch it on 'ere, put wool in 'ere, put dye in – an't wool comes out 'ere. We done it for years like this."

I just couldn't believe it – primitive wasn't the word for it.

"We'd thought about taking it to pieces – to make it easier to transport."

"Nay, bloody 'ell. I don't know that you can do that. I've been 'ere since I were a lad, but I don't know owt about tekin' it to pieces."

Further examination of the machine did nothing to increase my enthusiasm for the project. I said I'd let him know in the next few days what we'd decide.

"Well, Keith, are we going to be able to make use of it?" Mr Arkwright asked when I got back.

"I think, Mr Arkwright, you'd better come and have a look at it for yourself."

So I took him down to see for himself.

Just as I had done a week before, he looked in utter disbelief at this machine.

"What do you think of that then?" I asked, watching him closely to observe his reaction. "It's real, in't it? Shall I get the lads in to start taking it to pieces, then?"

He looked curiously at me.

"I'll tell you what," he said. "I think tradition is going to go out of the window today. We're going to find another firm, and that will have to do. Do you think anyone will notice if the cloth hasn't been dyed with the old machine?"

"Mr Arkwright," I said, "they won't have the slightest idea."

And from that day, we found another firm to do the dyeing. We called it 'indigo' and gave it the same code number, and, as far as I know, the top brass in the Forces have never twigged. For all these years they've been getting the natural indigo, and, suddenly, they started getting a new type of indigo. But there's been no phone call or letter yet to query our dyeing, so I suppose it can't be too bad.

Indigo was an exception to the general rule at Arkwright's, though. At Arkwright's, they firmly believed that, if a thing had been done for the past fifty years, then that was as good a reason as any for doing the same thing for the next fifty years. Thus, change came very slowly to the firm.

In the same way, it was tradition to make cloth from the same wool that we'd always made it from. One of the speciality cloths the mill made was a specific form of uniform cloth. This wool had to be of a special handle, and it was generally reckoned that the only wool suitable for making this particular uniform cloth came from the Wool Ranch, Queensland, Australia.

Each year the firm was desperately keen to have this cloth, and used to book a quantity to be sure of having it in stock and ready for use. No doubt they paid through the nose for it, but that didn't matter, of course.

The Australian farm from which the wool was bought went under the odd name of 'Cold Christmas Farm', but I've no idea why the owners gave it such an odd name.

One day I was called into the boss's office.

"Keith, we've got some VIPs coming today. I want you to show them around and look after them. They're particularly interested in the wool that they produce in Australia. They're from the 'Cold Christmas Ranch'. Make a big thing of it. Take them round the warehouse, and let them see how important their wool is to our operations."

It was a familiar routine I'd done many times before for guests to the mill.

Later that day, just after lunch, I was again summoned to the office; the VIPs had arrived. I was expecting to meet three or four hard-bargaining, dry-witted Australian businessmen, drawling in their customary laid-back style – the wool-exporting equivalent of Richie Benaud or Ian Chappell. Instead, I found myself offering my hand to two very old and very frail creatures, whose wizened faces spoke volumes of toil in the Australian countryside.

"Pleased to meet you, Keith," said one. "This is my wife, Vera. We're on holiday – first time in England, and we thought it would be sort of nice to see what happens to our wool."

"No problem," I replied. "I'll be pleased to show you."

We made our way rather slowly down to the warehouse, adjusting our eyes to the gloom of the building as we entered. We passed slowly by different bales of wool, piled high almost to the roof, until we arrived at the bales I knew belonging to 'Cold Christmas Ranch'.

"There you are," I said, pointing to this particular batch.

They both stood looking at them for some time. They must have seen hundreds of bales of wool in their time, and these were nothing different, except that these bales were their bales, all the way from their ranch in Queensland.

"Wonderful!" exclaimed the gentleman, warmly appreciating the importance of this spectacle.

"Isn't that really something!" added his wife. She must have been well into her eighties, and yet she enthused like someone very much younger.

"I tell you what," said the husband. "We'll take a photo of my wife standing on that bale. Come on, we'll get you standing on that bale."

He got his camera out and proceeded to make sure all was in order. Meanwhile, his wife was making a fair meal of clambering on to the first bale – not so easy for someone of advancing years. I gave her a helping push up, which I'm not sure was readily appreciated.

After some considerable struggle (and me trying not to burst out laughing at the incongruity of the well-dressed visitor perched precariously on top of this bale of wool), the photograph was taken, and I have not the slightest doubt that that photo will have been shown to all their friends and relatives back home in Australia for many years. It was the high spot of their once-in-a-lifetime trip, the day they saw their wool, from their very own farm, at Arkwright's, Yorkshire, England.

CHAPTER 7

Amidst all the goings-on at the mill, life was very hectic, it was a very busy mill. There was plenty of work, and the last thing anyone wanted was for somebody to throw a spanner in the works, or for the whole process to get snarled up. Then one day, quite out of the blue, a spanner came flying.

It came in the shape of Mr Arkwright himself, walking in with a new sports jacket.

"Now, then, what do you think of my new jacket?" he asked, doing a twirl the better for us to see. (Actually, the twirl made him stagger a little, as his body didn't quite respond to the sudden circular and unaccustomed motion.)

"Very nice, Mr Arkwright. It looks very smart," I replied, guardedly. I was a bit puzzled. The boss wasn't usually given to seeking compliments, but he was certainly pleased with my response. I'd obviously said the right thing this time.

"What do you think it's made of?" he asked, enigmatically.

"I ...er ...wool, I should think, Mr Arkwright."

"Not just wool, Keith," he said. "It's Jacob wool, Jacob wool. You've heard of Jacob wool, haven't you?"

"Er, no."

"Yes you have. Jacob... Jacob – from the Bible." (As if that explained everything.) "They're rare, are Jacob sheep, very rare."

"They must be."

"Extremely. I have a couple of aunts," he went on, "up in the Lake District; they breed these Jacob sheep."

"Really!"

"This jacket's made from Jacob wool, you know."

"That's very interesting, Mr Arkwright," I said, doing my best to ignore his drift, my mind, though, already beginning to foresee things it didn't want to see.

"Ay, lad, it is. I think," he continued, about to confirm my fears – we'd already more work on than we could handle – "I think we ought to make some Jacob yarn."

"Oh, my sainted aunt! " I muttered to myself.

"I thought you'd be impressed."

That wasn't how I saw my own reaction. Nevertheless...

"I've asked them to come down and see us – in fact, they're coming next week, and we're going to make some Jacob yarn."

That was all we needed. In the middle of all that was going on at the mill, the boss now wanted us to make Jacob yarn.

I said to him, "What's so special about this wool, then?"

"It's special," he replied, which did nothing to enlighten me. "It's spotted."

"Spotted?"

"Spotted – white sheep with brown spots, and white sheep with black spots. What we have to do is sort the black wool from the black spots, brown wool from the brown spots, and white from the background. When we've sorted it, we spin it. They're coming to see us next week."

(I'd gathered that the first time he'd said it.)

The following week, I couldn't believe it. With all the work we had in hand, and everybody rushing here, there and everywhere to get deliveries out the door, into the mill yard trundled a battered old Land Rover. It pulled up at the main door, and out stepped two ancient crones from the Lake District. The vehicle was full to the axle with their year's harvest of this Jacob wool.

After preliminary greetings and introductions, we turned to the subject of the Jacob wool.

"We go round to all the Shows," said one, "and we show our Jacob wool to lots of people, and everybody is absolutely thrilled with it. They say it's marvellous."

Her voice dwelt on the "mar" for emphasis. Maaarvellous.

"Really?"

"Oh, indeed. And Mr Arkwright says you can spin our wool for us."

"Yes, but what do we..."

"You have wool-sorters here, I understand?"

"Yes, we've..."

"Well, we'll show you how to do it."

"Listen to her, Keith," chipped in Mr Arkwright, who'd been standing with his hands behind his back all this while, with a fixed grin on his face, and a warm gleam in his eyes. "You can learn a lot by just listening to folk, you know. Just listen to 'em."

I think he could see that I was less than enthusiastic.

So we all lent a hand in getting this greasy wool out of the back of the Land Rover, brought it into the wool-sorting shed, and bunged it on the table.

My wool-sorters took one look at the wool, and went white.

"What in hell's name's this stuff?" one asked.

"It's Jacob wool."

"It's what?"

"Jacob wool – you know, Jacob – from the Bible. It's spotted. All you have to do is sort it – black from black spots, brown from the brown spots, and white from the background. That shouldn't be too difficult, should it?

"You're going to make sports jackets – like Mr Arkwright's. And smile while you're about it – these two ladies," I pointed to where they were standing some distance away, in earnest conversation with Mr Arkwright, "these two ladies are relatives of your boss; they're part of his family, so smile, and don't look so flaming miserable."

To an accompaniment of muttered threats and curses, the sorting of the wool began straightaway. It took three whole days of painstaking sorting. By the end of the first day, the wool-sorters were not speaking to me. By the end of the second, they were positively mutinous. The third day was not one I particularly wish to recall.

Eventually, we finished up with a bag of brown wool, a bag of black, a bag of white, and some very irritable sorters who had developed an intense dislike of Jacob sheep.

Mr Arkwright came in to see us just as we were finishing.

"You've got it sorted, then?"

His cheerfulness grated.

"Ay, we've done it. There's a bag of each there."

"Wonderful!" he exclaimed. "Wonderful! We'll get them spun up, and we'll make some sports jackets. They're going to take them to the Yorkshire Show, you know, and sell them."

"Wonderful!" I echoed.

"Yes," he continued, "they're going to put some sheep in a little pen next to the exhibition stand, and then everybody can see where it all comes from."

"Absolutely wonderful!" I exclaimed. "You get on with making the arrangements, Mr Arkwright, and we'll get it spun up." So I took the three bags of wool to the carding room.

"What the heck's that lot?" asked the carding engineer, with something less than civility, when he saw the contents of each bag.

"It's Jacob wool, Jacob wool; you know, Jacob - from the Bible. It's spotted. We've sorted it out. It's up to you to card it."

He, too, was not impressed. Carding machines need, on average, about half a ton of wool to be put in before you start getting anything out at the other end; here we had three bags with about a hundred kilos of wool in each, and when we'd emptied the three bags we'd barely even filled the hopper.

"What do you expect me to do with this lot?" asked the carding engineer in disgust.

"We're going to make some yarn, you know. We're then going to make it into sports jackets and show them at the Yorkshire Show, with sheep in a pen next to the stand."

He looked blankly at me.

"And don't look so flaming miserable. Just get on with it."

To say that the resulting cloth looked awful is a considerable understatement - it just did not gell. However, we eventually had some sports jackets made up, and the boss went to the Great Yorkshire Show, and stood at this Stand with his two elderly aunts, while all the sheep in the pen quietly nibbled all the grass and hay, and showed off this wonderful, wonderful wool.

"At least," I thought to myself, "that's the end of that, then. Thank goodness we've got rid of it."

Until, of course, sheep-shearing time came round again the following year.

"They're coming down again tomorrow," said Mr Arkwright one day, quite out of the blue.

"Who are, Mr Arkwright?" I asked, puzzled.

"My aunts - from the Lake District. You remember - last year?"

Could I forget.

"They're bringing us another load of Jacob wool. It's sheepshearing time, and they'll be on their way by morning. We made up some sports jackets. We'll have another go at that market."

I groaned inwardly. "If we've another three days of sorting like the first lot, the sorters will lynch me this time," I thought.

I puzzled for a long time what to do. Then it occurred to me that it was the summer holidays, and Joanne, our daughter, might just be interested in earning some money. Sixteen year old girls always need a bit extra pocket money for bits and pieces, I reasoned.

"Joanne, how do you fancy earning some pocket money?"

"What money will you pay me?" she asked, with a steady eye on priorities.

"Oh, I'll pay you a decent hourly rate for the job," I assured her and on the strength of that she agreed.

I took her down to the mill and announced that I had found someone to sort the Jacob wool, and the announcement was greeted by the sorters with a mixture of relief for themselves, and amazement that someone was actually prepared and willing to do the job.

When the sheer scale of the task dawned on her – within a few minutes of starting to sort the different colours – her willingness evaporated quickly, and it was sheer doggedness that got her through the next few miserable days. As she stood there, sorting the greasy black, white and brown wool into sacks, there was something akin to murder in her eyes.

To her credit, she stuck at it till the job was done, but, for some time after, anything I dared propose to her was greeted, on good days, with considerable doubt and suspicion – and open hostility on others!

Fortunately, before the next round of sheep-shearing and the visit of the battered Land Rover, I got the urge once more to move on.

CHAPTER 8

You looked for jobs in the *Yorkshire Post*; there were always plenty of jobs advertised, and one, in particular, caught my eye. Standish & Co.

To cut a long story short, I was pretty pleased with myself when, after two interviews, I was offered the job as mill manager by Walter Standish, manager and owner of Standish & Co.

I went back to Arkwright's that same afternoon and handed in my notice.

"You leaving? What are you going for?" asked Mr Arkwright.

"Well, one or two reasons, but, mainly, I think I need a new challenge, Mr Arkwright," I said, failing utterly to put into adequate words my desire to try 'pastures new'.

"Where are you going to?" he enquired. I told him I'd got the job of mill manager at Standish's.

His eyes widened in amazement.

"You're joking!" he said.

"No; I start at the beginning of next month."

Then he started to laugh. A very rueful sort of laugh.

"You've seen the place, have you?"

"Of course. I've had two interviews."

I hadn't, actually, having been interviewed in the local Commercial club.

"I'm telling you, Keith, it's a heck of a place to work in, if what I hear is true. If I were you, I'd give it a bit more serious thought."

"Oh, I don't think so, Mr Arkwright. I've made up my mind. I've been very happy here, and there are lots of reasons why I should stay, but I think I need a change of scene. That's the only reason for leaving."

"Well, you know your own mind. If things don't work out, just let me know, will you."

I thanked him and told him I would. You don't leave a place run by somebody like Mr Arkwright without a great many misgivings – and regrets. Especially when you don't really know what you're moving on to.

The winter nights were drawing in, as I came to the end of my month's notice. I decided it might not be a bad idea to have a look at the premises where I would be working shortly.

"Fancy taking a job, and I haven't even seen the place," I said to myself. "I must be barmy."

I had no idea what I was letting myself in for.

If what Mr Arkwright had hinted was true – about the condition of the mill – I thought I might be in for a bit of a shock.

However, I was pleasantly surprised when I finally got there. From a distance it didn't look too bad.

It seemed a bit odd, and I remember thinking so at the time, that here I was, newly appointed as mill manager, creeping like some wretched sneak-thief into the yard to see where I was going to be working.

I peered round the brick gateway into the mill yard. The sight that presented itself to me confirmed my worst fears and shattered any illusions that it wasn't going to be 'too bad'.

Putting it mildly, the place was in a terrible mess. It was as if the proverbial bomb had struck – but several years before.

All was dirt, and rubbish, and rubble, and papers, and years of neglect.

There were broken boxes; there were torn, hessian-covered massive bales of yarn; there were clusters of loose, white, greasy wool blowing gently across the yard; they clung to everything they touched, sticky as seaside candyfloss. Patched and crumbling tarmac exposed light-grey setts tinged with bright green moss. What a sight! My heart sank as I saw it. Even so, there was now no going back. This was where my own particular caravan was going to rest for a while at least.

A few days before I was due to finish at Arkwright's, I rang Walter Standish, and we arranged to meet. Leaving work early, I made my way across town to Standish Mills, parked the car, and picked my way through the debris to the main office. I knocked on the door.

"Mr Haigh? Ah, yes," said a young, dark-haired – very striking – receptionist, politely. "Mr Standish has been delayed. Would you like to come upstairs to the boardroom?"

She smiled, as she stepped in front of me, to lead me along a short corridor, then up a flight of dusty stone steps, her elegant but practical black shoes clicking on each tread as she lightly ascended the stairs.

We reached a solid wooden door, and she smiled again as I pushed it open for her to bring us on to another corridor. Immediately opposite was the door to the boardroom. She, in her turn, pushed open the door, invited me to enter, and left me on my own in the gloom.

A brief recollection of the light from Estella's candle disappearing down the stairs, as Pip was left to meet Miss Havisham, flitted through my mind. Unforgettable Jean Simmons.

I made my way past the heavy mahogany table filling the middle of the room, to the tall sash windows on the far side. I could see down into the yard below.

There was a chill in the air, and a sudden puff of the breeze made leaves on the ground come to life; for a few brief moments they danced a drunken dance, and died as quickly as they had come to life. I continued to peer out of the grimy window of the boardroom, and shifted my gaze to the distant rounded spine of the Pennines.

Here I was again, I thought. Another new beginning. What lies in store for me this time? I waited with some degree of anticipation the introduction to the next phase of my life.

I'd hardly taken stock of my surroundings when the door behind me burst suddenly open and in strode Walter Standish.

He greeted me warmly, like an old acquaintance. His handshake was firm and solid. In his youth he'd probably been very good-looking; the chin and jaw were sharply etched, though passing years had added several creases. Fair hair, now going grey, and fair eyebrows gave his face character. He was tall, slim, with a wiry sort of stature – the sort that you'd expect to find in a good high-jumper, and there was a sort of nervous energy in his movements, as though he needed to be up and doing.

In no time at all, I was following him briskly down the same dimly lit corridor I had traversed a few minutes earlier, as he began to show me round his mill – and now my mill, too.

The place was indeed as rundown as one can possibly imagine.

We went round, meeting and greeting everybody as we went. It was a cool, fresh day, but I well recall, as we hurried into the wool-scouring room, the pungent smell of the wool and the steam that rose in clouds from the huge scouring machines. I should have been repelled by this acrid stench that met my nostrils, but there was something – it is difficult to put into words – something vaguely appealing. I don't mean that I relished this place – far from it; but there was something about the atmosphere, and the steady throb of the vast machines, and the quiet, purposeful attention of the workers to their allotted tasks, that made me feel comfortable with the decisions I'd made years ago to find my way in this particular industry. This world of noise and grime, and the sharp smells of oil and wet wool, are oddly reassuring and soothing.

Working at Standish & Co. proved to be very different from the world I'd worked in before – as I knew it would be. Here was a new challenge, and within a few short, hectic weeks, the set-up became clear to me.

The name of the game was survival. Forget the conditions – get on with the job. You'd been appointed to do a job, don't bother telling Walter Standish your problems – he wasn't interested – just get the job done.

Having said that, I soon learned that if there were any problems or disputes with people outside the mill (and there were plenty), he'd back you to the hilt, right or wrong. I've known some bosses who wouldn't lift a finger to help you in a crisis.

My new boss was a bit of an odd beggar. There was more than a streak of business ruthlessness in him, and he lost no opportunity in telling people what he thought of them, if things weren't right. He could cut people down to size with just a few well-chosen words, and quite a number of employees smarted under the effect of his sharp tongue. Very blunt, very down-to-earth. A bit 'brussen', as we say.

Perhaps that was the way he'd been brought up to deal with people, or, maybe, that was his method of coming to terms with the tricky world he inhabited. I don't know.

He was about my own age, and, perhaps for this reason, we managed to get along fairly amicably much of the time. We shared quite a lot of views on how the mill should be run. That, at least, made life a little easier for me than it otherwise might have been. He seemed to appreciate having someone to act as a sounding board for his ideas.

The mill itself was falling to bits, the machinery was unreliable, but if you knew your job and could achieve the results, you could survive in Walter Standish's world. This often entailed doing a lot of things you didn't like doing, but you just had to get on and do them.

The chap who'd had the job before me was unlucky. I'd known him since college days, and the job had broken him; he hadn't been able to cope with the pressure of the job, and there's no doubt that Walter was a hard taskmaster.

On the other hand, the workers were quite well paid, but working in almost impossible conditions. It wasn't surprising that they were very militant and out to cause as much hassle as they could. I quickly learned that you had to stand your ground with them, or they'd eat you for lunch. You had to get what you wanted out of them as best you could.

With Walter Standish on one side, and the workers on the other, my job was not easy.

If the impression has been given that money was not spent if it could possibly be avoided, that is pretty near the truth. Making a working profit in the textile trade took ingenuity, hard work and risks. Everything was done (or not done) with economy in mind. There was no time for making things merely look good.

At this time, the mill possessed some ancient spinning frames – an old type that had started their working life at Benton & Co. – one of the mills up the road, not far from Standish's. These spinning frames were being scrapped, but when Walter Standish heard of this, he bought them at auction, on condition that he would dismantle them and take them away.

Benton's had already run these machines night and day for many years, and they believed that they were absolutely beyond repair. When fitters came in from Standish's, Benton's works engineer couldn't believe his eyes.

"What the heck you doing?" he asked, amazed.

"Numbering all the parts, so as we can put these machines up again at t'other end," came the reply.

"You mean to say you're going to put 'em up again? They're jiggered, them machines."

"Na, the's years o' life in 'em yet."

The systematic dismantling went ahead, as planned, and before long they were up and running at our mill.

To put this move into perspective, Benton's have replaced their machinery twice in the same period of time. But that's how Standish survived, and others less thrifty have gone under.

I'd been at Standish's a year or so. It was summer and Walter Standish decided that the dyehouse could manage no longer with its present roof. Rain poured in from various points, and a new roof had become absolutely essential. In the dyehouse was a yarn-scouring plant, and the process worked like this.

Hanks of yarn were fed into large, open bowls, and were transferred from one bowl to another. The hot water and soap in each bowl washed the yarn, and, as the hanks were transferred, less and less detergent was used in each bowl, until the last bowl was simply clear, clean water, to wash off any remaining detergent.

The hanks were then fed through squeeze rollers at the end, and then one of the operatives would put them on a feed sheet, which would take the yarn into a drying machine. This machine contained a big chamber through which hot air was blown until the hanks were dry.

The whole process from start to finish was a three-man operation - two feeding in, and the third transferring the hanks to the drying machine,

If the machinery was in a poor state, the building itself was in far worse state. A new roof was many years overdue. Walter, however, never brought contractors in to do any job his own men might to able to do

"Right," he announced, one early summer morning. "What we'll do is take the roof off in the summer holidays, and put a new one on in the autumn by working overtime and weekends."

That was all there was to it. It all sounded fine. The theory was good. Sure enough, two weeks of glorious sunshine and warm weather, and the roof was off. The yarn-scouring room was open to the elements, and the sun continued to shine, bathing the workers down below in late summer sunshine.

Weeks went by, and autumn crept in - still no sign of a move to put on the new roof.

"What's happening about the new roof to the yarn-scouring room?" I asked at one of our meetings.

"That's not for you to worry about," said Walter, a bit sharply. "That's my problem. You just get on with your job."

I tentatively broached the subject from time to time, but Walter didn't want to know.

November arrived, and the air in the scouring room was distinctly chill. Steam from the bowls blended well with morning mists and afternoon fog.

Christmas came and went, and, then, in January, it began to snow.

You had to admire the men, working as normal. They huddled round the bowls for warmth; they were dressed in woolly hats, scarves, heavy overcoats on top of thick, woollen sweaters, and were slowly being covered in a fine layer of snow. There was something almost reminiscent of Pompeii in their fortitude and staunch resistance to the elements. Perhaps Nanouk of the North fitted their state more aptly, as they continued to work in Arctic conditions.

Snow, by this time, was over their boots, and how the workers managed to keep going I shall never know. It was like working in a field. Ice on the machines also began to cause problems.

Then, one beautiful winter afternoon, with weak sunlight disappearing behind a thick mass of grey-black clouds, a car drew up outside the main office, and a young, fresh-faced chap stepped out into the snow-covered yard. He knocked on the door, came in, tapping the snow from his shoes.

"My name's Peter Jackson," he said, cheerily. "I'm the new factory inspector, and I've come to do the annual inspection."

I could see straightaway some interesting developments in this unannounced visit.

"I see. You'd better come this way."

By now, a blizzard was blowing.

"How do you wish to proceed?" I asked.

"Well, I'd just like to look round the factory, see that the working conditions are up to standard – usual sort of thing," he replied.

We set off round the factory, the inspector very efficient-looking with his clipboard and biro. He peered around as we walked, stopping every now and then to make notes, and then walking on.

We got through the blending department, which was a bit of a tip, to say the least.

"Er, this machine, it's quite old, isn't it'?"

He could say that again!

"I think it should have a safety guard here, and one here, and one..." He looked more closely. "You know, string isn't allowed."

"What?" I exclaimed in mock horror. "We use a lot of string. In fact, it's the main commodity. String keeps everything going in this place."

It was intended as a joke, but it wasn't so far from the truth! He didn't see the joke at all. He just tut-tutted and carried on.

"Well, it's not very good. I shall have to make a few notes."

And then we turned a corner, and we shuffled into the scouring room. Well, it wasn't a room now – more like a yard.

He stood in the doorway and looked across this 'yard', and through the snow of the blizzard, to the steam rising from the bowls of the yarn-scouring tanks, to the drier belching out volleys of steam, and to these three eskimo-like figures bending down, intent upon their work, in a sort of silent communion – silent because they were too cold to speak. A sudden flurry of wind whipped up eddies of snow above their boots, whilst gentle puffs of snow fell from the men's woolly hats and hoods.

For a while, there was a strange silence all round the room, broken only by the muffled thud of the men stamping their feet for warmth.

The inspector looked at the men, looked at me, then looked back again to the men in utter disbelief.

"Er," he turned to me again, "can you tell me what this department is, please?"

"It's the yarn-scouring department."

"But there's no... er... roof..." He pointed skywards with his biro.

"No," I replied, seriously. "But we do intend to put one on in the not-too-distant future," I said, "when money becomes available. So I understand. So Mr Standish tells me. It could be fairly imminent, in fact."

Obviously, no coherent response occurred to him at that moment. Then he came back to life. "Do you mind if I have a word with these operatives?"

"By all means," I said.

He approached two of the men, and bent his face low to peer into their hooded faces.

"Excuse me," he said to the one nearest to him, "do you normally operate this machine in these conditions?" The young chap looked at him in surprise.

"I only wear mi 'ood when it's snowin'," he said, slightly on the defensive. Here was someone you didn't treat lightly. The inspector didn't say anything.

The young chap sniffed, and drew a thick-coated wrist across his nose.

"I've got to wear mi 'ood when it's snowin'," the man went on, just in case he'd not been heard. "If I don't, mi 'air gets wet."

The inspector nodded and turned away. He had definitely heard, and seemed to lapse into a daydream, a kind of dazed reverie. It didn't take much to know what was going through his head at that moment.

We walked back to the office in silence.

"Well, would you like to come into my office and discuss the factory?" I asked, as we reached the door.

"Er..." he stammered for a second, striving to bring his thoughts together. "If it's alright with you, I'll get on my way now."

"Fine."

"I'll send my report as soon as I can," he added.

We shook hands, and I watched him to his car. Looking out of the window some ten minutes later, I could see his car was still there, and he was sitting motionless inside.

After about a quarter of an hour, the car door abruptly opened, and he strode purposefully back to the office door, knocked and walked in.

"Mr Haigh," he said, "I've just been writing up my notes on the mill. Quite frankly," he said, "I can't believe what I've written. Can you just check that what I've written is true?"

Sure enough, when, about a month later, the report came through, it was not unlike a condensed version of the Encyclopaedia Britannica, and a veritable mine of observations regarding what the inspector thought was wrong with the mill. They gave us three months to put things right, as they always used to do. The yarn-scouring department was picked out for special mention. Surprise!

Typically, nothing happened, and it was months before Standish got round to putting a roof on the yarn-scouring room. The operatives deserved a medal for their fortitude and endurance.

The absence of a roof was obviously a bit special, but leaking roofs were a perennial problem that the mill endured every time it rained.

The workers would complain – naturally – and a militant union was led by a woman who would have made a good soul-mate for Attila in her fierce opposition to the management. She was a real tyrant, and ruled the twisting department like some latter-day Boadicea. Woe betide any of the workers who crossed swords with her when she was in pursuit of her union duties.

My days seem to have been taken up with running skirmishes – and sometimes pitched battles – with this union virago.

Somehow, there had to be a compromise between meeting her demands, on the one hand, and making sure I got the work through, on the other. It was often touch and go.

One particularly heavy downpour one day brought a volley of complaints from one of the girls working at one of the twisting frames. She complained bitterly that rain was dripping from a hole in the roof on to her head. It was very disturbing, and annoying, to be working at her twisting frame and have water running down her neck; she couldn't concentrate, she said.

Here was obviously a case for action, before the union got hold of the problem and brought things to a halt.

Walter Standish was deep into a pile of papers on his desk when he motioned me to enter.

"Mr Standish," I said, "something needs to be done, urgently. We can't have the workers getting soaked whilst they're working. It's not right. There's rain getting in all over the place."

I could see he wasn't interested. He continued leafing through papers as he spoke.

"Don't give me your problems," he said, without looking up. "I've enough to be doing. Sort it out yourself. Give her an umbrella or something."

He plainly didn't wish to know at that moment how close the twisting department was to strike action. I left his office, wondering what to do.

The rain continued pelting down. I had to do something. Then it occurred to me that I had, in fact, an umbrella in the car.

I dashed over to the car park, took out the umbrella, and, without a second thought, holding the umbrella behind me, I strode down to the twisting department.

I walked down the middle of the mill and reached the frame where she was working. She was getting very agitated.

Without saying a word, I produced the umbrella from behind me, opened it up, and handed it to her.

She took one look, saw the look on my face, and collapsed in a fit of laughter. It was the best thing that could have happened, as it turned out, and defused a situation that could have been unpleasant, not to say, unproductive.

So, fortunately, she saw the funny side of the situation. She knew I had a problem, too. We didn't get the roof repaired, but at least we were able to have a laugh about it – for the time being – and Attila's mate knew nothing about it. The mill carried on production.

If you can remember the 'Rag Trade', in the early days of television, starring Miriam Karlin, you might begin to have an idea of conditions as they were at Standish Mills.

In comparison with some other jobs, these girls were quite well paid, but they deserved to be. It wasn't a sinecure. With such bad working conditions to contend with, the women seemed to threaten me with strike action about once a month. Fortunately for me, they rarely carried out their threat.

One particular winter evening, the nightwatchman telephoned to say that he couldn't start up the boiler. As it was essential to get up the heat for the morning shift, I immediately called out the engineer and arranged to meet him at the mill.

It was in the early hours of the morning when we finally got the boiler to work. It was always a tricky job, especially as Walter Standish saw little point in getting it serviced till it actually went wrong.

By the time the day shift was due to arrive, we'd managed to get some warmth into the mill, but hardly what you'd call 'working temperature'.

Having been working most of the night, I decided to go home for my breakfast and be back in time for the start of the morning shift.

When I arrived back at the mill, I was met at the gate.

"We've got a deputation and we're here to tell you that we're going out on strike."

It was Brenda Forsyth, Attila's mate, leading the deputation. Her jaw was set, and I could see she meant business this time. Nothing but a good show of solidarity to produce a strike would suit her.

"It states in the manual that the temperature for working in the mill should be at an agreed level before we start work. The temperature at this moment in the mill is three degrees below our agreed level, so we're going on strike."

I felt a little aggrieved. I'd been up most of the night getting the boiler to work, but neither argument nor persuasion tempted the union to move from its stance. More to the point, the firm was not well placed to withstand a stoppage.

I went into my office. She followed me in.

"We're going home," she said, in a very matter-of-fact tone, "and under the conditions of our employment you've got to pay us a morning's wage until the heat comes up."

She stood there, with her arms crossed, to let what she had just said sink in.

"But..." I began.

"She's right, you know," bleated a little chap, another union official, standing insignificantly beside her. "You'll have to pay."

With that, the damage done, they turned on their heels and began to file out.

"Just a minute," I called out to them. I'd no idea what we could do this time. They certainly had right on their side, and I'd have to accept the situation. They'd got me on this occasion.

"I'll call a meeting for two o'clock," I announced.

"It won't make any difference," she said, scenting undisputed victory. "You'll still have to pay us, you know."

And on that note she walked out.

So, here was a tricky problem which needed a great deal of careful thought – and quickly – before the afternoon shift arrived.

As I was thinking, I stood, gazing out of my office window. At the mill gate, I could see huddled groups of women engaged in earnest conversation. Around them fretted their children, eager to be on the move.

At that moment, the solution occurred to me.

The women, at this time, had a kind of syndicate of caring for each other's babies and children. Those on the afternoon shift looked after the children of the women working the morning shift, and vice versa.

Who said life was easy for these women? Each day was a trial of strength and stamina. To work a full shift, doing a repetitive and often tedious job, then to do the shopping, or pick up the children from school, or go home and start the washing and ironing, and the cleaning, and making a full dinner for their husband when he came home from work, whilst all the time keeping an eye on the children – it was a routine which demanded more of women than they should be asked to give. No doubt I should have campaigned harder to lighten their load – but I had a mill to run.

That was the problem. The livelihoods of a lot of families depended on the steady output of the mill. That had to come first. If production stopped, or we became uncompetitive, there was no one there to bail us out; we had to stand on our own.

Two o'clock. The mill yard filled up. There was a general buzz of animated conversation. These women knew their rights, and they meant business – for three degrees of warmth.

The meeting was brief. The militant unionist re-stated her position, and this was greeted with a chorus of approval. There was a lot of chatter, and some good-natured heckling from the back, followed by shrill laughter.

"Right," I said. "You've made your point pretty clear. You shouldn't have to work in temperatures below our agreed figure."

They nodded their approval to each other; they had fought their case, and had won. Brenda's eyes gleamed as she turned to smile at the ones closest to her.

"I think I've now solved the problem," I went on. "There shouldn't be any need for strike action now. What I propose to do is alter the times of the shifts.

Starting tomorrow, the morning shift will begin at eleven o'clock. The afternoon shift will also begin three hours later than at present. This will give ample time for the mill to heat up, so you should be warm enough from now on."

"Can you do that?" asked Brenda, her face rapidly losing its smugness.

"Yes, I can do that. It's in the manual," I said, quietly.

There was silence all round.

The next few days were chaotic. I knew that the mothers were all finding difficulty in getting babysitters for their children.

At the beginning of the fourth day of the new system, there was a knock on my door.

"Come in," I called out. Brenda shuffled in.

"Mr Haigh, we've decided."

"Yes?"

"We'd, maybe, stand it being a bit cold now and again, if we can go back to the old shift times."

She looked me straight in the eyes. The truculence of the other day had been replaced by a dead-pan dullness in her look.

"I don't think that will present too many problems," I answered.

She knew that this time she had lost out, but there would be other times.

The daily routine of these young women seems to make them old before their time, and every line on their faces betrays the harshness of their lives. Life shouldn't have to be so tough.

CHAPTER 9

I stuck it out at Standish Carpets for several years – more's the wonder, considering the poor conditions in which all of us worked. But the time came when I realised I didn't want to spend the rest of my working life there. My many years of grafting in mills across the country told me there were better pastures still to graze in.

Within a couple of weeks or so of thinking about moving on, my eyes lit upon an advertisement for a wool buyer. It was for a firm I'd heard of but didn't know a great deal about. For some unaccountable reason, the timing once again seemed to be right for chance to beckon me on.

It must have been October when I was called for interview. A warm, autumnal glow cast long, lazy shadows on the grey stone pavements, and bathed them in a subtle warmth, as I parked my car and walked, for the first time, into Benton's Mill.

Even at first glance, I was struck by the cleanness of the place, the tidy white paintwork on the window frames, the sandblasted stonework, and everything looking in good order. The mill had been built about 1905, but how well it had been cared for over the years. I suppose, my having spent years at Standish's, any improvement would have been noticeable, but this place was certainly in a different class.

I was met at reception by a man who, I reckon, would have been in his sixties but who looked much younger. There was genuine warmth in his greeting that made me take to him straightaway. He introduced himself as Edgar Peters.

"Mr Haigh?"

"Yes," I replied.

"Mr Benton said you'd be coming this morning. I'll show you to his office."

In the years that followed, Edgar Peters, who worked as the colour matcher, was to become a close working companion; he was superb at his job, and, as a person, was as steady as a rock – the sort of person, in fact, the phrase 'salt of the earth' was made for. There don't come any better.

As we walked along a well-lit corridor, I could see into the testing laboratory. Everything was clean and tidy, and the rooms breathed an air of quiet efficiency.

We reached the offices, then paused in front of a door near the far end. Edgar knocked and walked in.

"I've got Mr Haigh here, Mr Benton," said Edgar, as I followed him into quite a large, carpeted office.

"Ah, do come in."

Mr Peters beckoned me in. A slim, fairly tall, grey-haired gentleman stood up, and proffered a hand. We shook hands and he motioned me to sit down. Between us was a beautiful mahogany table half-hidden beneath papers.

I was looking at a man not a great deal older than myself. I could see immediately that, in the nicest way, he was what I would have called one of the 'old school' of mill owners. I mean that he was softly spoken, had a most amiable and unassuming manner, and a disarming smile that put you at your ease, yet combined these qualities with a very businesslike and down-to-earth directness.

Is it the industry they are in that produces men of this character? Or are such men drawn to this industry? I don't know, but meeting such men, as I have done through my life, has been a source of much pleasure and continued admiration for their qualities.

"Will you have a cup of tea, Mr Haigh? I'm just about to have one myself."

I said that I would, and thanked him. He busied himself with cups and saucers, giving me time to look around.

He himself was smartly dressed in a charcoal grey, pinstripe suit, striped shirt, and very subdued tie. But his office, which I took in with one sweep, was as if it had just been burgled. There were books and papers and files and catalogues and bills in no particular order scattered round – the only place on his desk for two cups of tea was on top of half a dozen books, and there they stayed, perched precariously, until I rescued one of them, and Mr Benton took the other on to his lap. We sort of peered at each other over the books for a second or two.

"Now, then, Mr Haigh, thank you very much for coming. Shall we just have a chat for a while, then I'll show you round?"

He talked about his family, showed me photos of them, spoke about his brother, co-owner of the mill, who was hoping to retire. What Mr Benton now required was someone to take over some of the responsibility of running the mill. The position on offer was obviously a key post.

In return, I talked about the years I'd spent in the mills, the jobs I'd done, leading up to the present. He sat and listened intently, especially when I touched upon my years working for Bill Lister and Brian Porter up at Appleyard's – it seemed an age ago.

An hour soon went by, and it was good to be able to talk to someone who knew the industry as intimately as Mr Benton did. I felt perfectly at ease in these surroundings. Now and again he'd nod agreement or smile, and from time to time, would ask a question.

At the end of this hour - the tea had gone cold – he took me round and showed me the mill at work. I could not fail to be impressed. Here was a mill of the eighties – not the thirties – an up-to-the-minute unit that anyone would be proud to be part of. The machinery was superb, and, nice to see, most of them were British made. He bought foreign machines only when absolutely necessary.

I already knew that I'd give my eye teeth to work in such a place. There couldn't have been a bigger contrast between where I worked and where I'd like to work.

"Well," he said at last. "Thanks for coming. I've a lot of people to see, but I'll let you know as soon as I can. It's been very pleasant talking to you, especially your working with Brian so long ago. You know, Brian's an old friend of mine – we were at university together."

I thought, "I knew it. I knew there was some tie-up between them." It was just as well that I'd spoken about Brian in such complimentary terms – not that I would have ever said anything derogatory about Brian – but I could tell it seemed to strike a chord between Graham Benton and myself; we had a source of mutual affinity – or some such phrase.

Graham also knew a great deal about others I'd worked with in the past. I suppose it was only to be expected. He probably knew more about myself than I did!

"I don't know whether I'll need you back for a second interview, Mr Haigh. I've still a lot of people to see," he repeated.

"Well, thank you very much, Mr Benton." We shook hands again, very formally, but I thought I could detect it was more than just a dismissive gesture.

"I'll look forward to hearing from you."

In fact, I heard nothing for quite a long time – long enough for me to begin to put the thought of working at Benton's out of my mind.

Perhaps, I reasoned, I'm not going to be lucky this time. Plenty of people would be pleased to work at a mill like that. I'd just about given up when, one day, I got a phone call.

"Graham Benton here. I wonder if you'd like to come over and have another chat?"

I arranged to see him after work the following week, and it wasn't long before I was again sitting opposite him, just as before, peering over the books on the mahogany table. It was a bitterly cold, crisp November evening outside, but, here, in the office, it was warm and relaxing.

"Will you have a cup of tea, Mr Haigh?"

He always liked to start things off in the right way.

"I don't think it will surprise you to know that I've been talking to Brian. I hope you don't mind?"

"Not at all, Mr Benton."

"He thinks very highly of you. So, as things are…" This sounded very promising. My luck might be in after all. "…and, subject to an agreement between us…" I was already anticipating his next words, and I could feel a sense of pleasure welling up inside me.

"…I'd like to offer you a post as my assistant here."

He looked at me steadily.

"Well… er… thank you very much, Mr Benton. I very much appreciate it."

I certainly did. The thought of working in these surroundings filled me with anticipated pleasure. What a change this would make to my life.

"Now, then," he went on. "Shall we get down to the nitty-gritty?"

I could feel myself grinning inside – even after so many years and so many interviews. I was like a kid again with a new Christmas toy.

"Before you start here, I'll get you a company car."

I'd only once had a company car before. This was a bonus. "And shall we say as your starting salary…" He named a figure. My hopes dried up like a prune. I suppose I should have realised earlier that he didn't obtain a mill in that condition by being unnecessarily philanthropic.

"You realise, of course, with buying you a company car, I'm not able to offer you as much as, perhaps, you would like." He was not offering even half as much as I'd have liked! Realistically, the sum was well below what I was already earning at Standish's.

Certainly, the working conditions, the experience and job satisfaction counted for a great deal. It was a hard decision.

"I'm sorry, Mr Benton," I said, after a while. "I can't accept your offer.'

"Ah; I thought you might be surprised," he said. "But times are hard in this industry, you know."

"Yes; I do know, Mr Benton, but I've got a family and a mortgage."

How many times must prospective employers have heard that!

"Well, then, let's just discuss the position for a while."

And we did. We argued our points of view over another cup of tea that also went cold, and, eventually – and, I think, to the relief of both of us – we reached a compromise, and I accepted.

Details such as these are not important in the general run of life, but I record them for what they are – milestones in the path of a life that had meandered a long way from its point of origin – not in miles, but in experience and knowledge.

My official title was 'wool buyer' – not a particularly startling title to show for so many years in the industry. Oddly enough, in all the years I worked at Benton's, I didn't do much wool-buying. Mind you, I did just about every other job there was to do.

Shortly after I'd accepted the position, I was talking with a couple of my contacts in the business. Obviously I told them I'd got a new job and was about to start work at Benton's.

"Bloody hell!" said one of them, not mincing his words. "I suppose you know what you've let yourself in for?"

I could feel a kind of chill suddenly catch me by the throat.

"Not again," I said to myself. I'd heard these words before.

"Why? What do you mean?" I asked.

"There's two brothers there, you know. One of them's a right old beggar! If he's still there, and the other one's the one who's retired, you're in a right mess, Keith," he said. "He'll make your life an absolute misery," he added, ominously. "He's a right so-and-so."

He didn't elaborate any further on the subject, but he made it pretty clear that I was in for a rough ride, if, indeed, I'd drawn the short straw with the wrong brother. For a moment or two, the seeds of doubt were sown. But then I recalled the conversations I'd already had with the boss, and I was pretty sure – and relieved – that the right brother had stayed on to manage the firm. Subsequently, that proved to be the case, fortunately.

A surprise flurry of January snow whirled around me as I was dropped off at the door of the mill for my first day at Benton's. I'd no car, so Philippa had ferried me down in her little car, but I knew that I would be picking up my company car later in the day. It made me feel quite important.

This impression was reinforced when I walked into reception. Prying eyes and curious people hung around, wanting to catch a first glimpse of the person who would be wielding quite a bit of power in the mill – or so it seemed to me at the time. Quite heady stuff, this illusion of power! Fortunately, I was old enough to recognise it for what it was – just an illusion.

I announced myself

"Ah, yes, Mr Haigh: Mr Benton is expecting you. He won't be a minute. Please take a seat."

Shortly after, even before I'd begun to take stock of my surroundings, Graham Benton bustled in.

"Good morning, Keith. Would you like to come this way. I've just got to go through my post and then I'll be with you. But I'll show you to your office first. I'll have a cup of tea sent to you. Have you a newspaper to read for a few minutes?"

"Yes, Mr Benton. I've got my *Yorkshire Post*." The remark sounded almost like the first line of an advertising blurb!

I followed him along the corridor I'd first travelled for my interviews.

"Here you are," he said. We entered quite a large, well-lit, airy room. "I hope you'll be alright here. Just give me a few minutes, and we'll get things sorted out."

Even at first glance, I couldn't fail to be impressed. Carpet on the floor, beautiful mahogany desk, swivel chair, tasteful paintings on the walls, executive toilet. Executive toilet! I suppose many people have come to this stage in their working careers and not thought a great deal about it. For me, it had been a long, hard road; I'd taken more of the rough than the smooth on the way, and there'd been many a time when I doubted whether I'd ever get anywhere in my life.

Here, now, for the first time, I began to take stock of my situation and felt proud of what I'd achieved – and grateful, too, to all those who'd helped me achieve it.

It's a funny kind of feeling, and somehow very satisfying – not that sort of smug 'Look-at-me-aren't-I-clever' type of feeling; more like: 'Aren't I lucky to be the one who managed to get to the top of a business which I also enjoy.' I allowed myself the indulgence of a few moments' daydreaming.

Attached to the office was the wool room. I opened the heavy, mahogany door and peered in. This was where I would be working from now on.

All the wool samples were neatly arranged in pigeon holes along the walls and up to the ceiling, each sample with its own label on the front of the polished wood of the shelves.

I knew that I'd enjoy working here.

Returning to my office, I'd just sat down to drink my tea, when the door from the corridor burst open abruptly, and in strode a tall, elderly man. He was obviously as surprised to see me as I was to see him. One look told me that this must be the other brother who had retired from the firm.

"Good morning!" I said, cheerfully.

"Who the bloody hell are you?" he snarled, with a scowl on his face. There was no doubting his unfriendliness.

"I've just been appointed as the new wool buyer."

I stood up to introduce myself, but thought better of it. I didn't see why I should be intimidated by this man whom I assumed to be the other Mr Benton – I was working for his brother, not him.

"And, if it isn't a rude question, who the bloody hell are you?"

He grunted, and walked past me into the wool room. I could hear him putting things in a case. Obviously, he was still clearing out his belongings, stuff that he'd left behind when he'd moved out the week before.

After a while he shuffled back into the office.

"I know all about you," he said, pointing a bony finger in my direction. "You won't last two minutes in this job; you don't know enough about this side of the business."

He turned round, and, without another word or look, disappeared out of the office.

"Great! Nice chap!" I thought. Well, what I actually thought was tinged with rather more Anglo-Saxon.

Eventually, just as I was composing a suitable remark, should he come back in again, Mr Benton – my boss – breezed in. "Now, then, Keith, we can make a start."

He pulled up a chair to sit facing me.

"I think I've just met your brother," I blurted out.

"Oh." There was silence for a few moments. "What did he say to you?"

"Nothing much, really. Just that I wouldn't last very long in this job, because I don't know enough about this side of the business."

"Well," said Mr Benton, "don't take any notice of him. We've never quite got on together, and he's getting a bit crusty in his old age. I don't think he's sure even now whether he's glad to be retiring or not. We've worked hard in this firm over the years, and I think it's just getting a bit topside of him. It's a wrench, you know, leaving a firm you've given your life to."

"I can appreciate that," I said. All the same, I was happy to know that I wouldn't be seeing much of him in the future. Even on such short acquaintance I had very definite opinions on the retiring Mr Benton.

My first instincts about Benton's Mill were borne out in practice over the next few months. I settled in well, enjoyed the company of my colleagues, and seemed to get on well with most people. It was pleasant employment, and I soon learned to put behind me the recollections of the conditions we'd all worked under at Standish's. I was out and away from that place, but I had much sympathy for those still there. However, time dims the memory.

I also got on well with Graham Benton, and he proved to be a man whose judgment I could trust, even if I didn't always agree with him. He didn't have a lot of patience, if he thought you should know something about your job and you didn't – he could be curt and off-hand in these situations, and rightly so; you were expected to know your job.

As managing director, and chairman of a company, a person should know a great deal about business and how to run a firm, or so you would expect, but it was often the case that M.D.s had little more than just a vague idea of the technical side of the business.

I had gained this impression of Graham Benton. One day, however, the carding engineer came striding into Graham's office whilst we were in the middle of a meeting.

This carding engineer had worked in this mill since he'd left school; indeed, his father and grandfather had worked there for most of their working lives – it was the tradition, just as it was with many families in this locality.

"Mr Benton, that new blend you've given me for No. 3 machine is hopeless."

He was obviously quite agitated.

"It won't go at all," he went on. " It's useless."

"What seems to be the matter?" said Mr Benton.

"It won't go, that's what the matter is; it's short wool and it just won't run. It's fouling up the machine."

His voice grew steadily louder and more irritable as he spoke.

"Don't get so upset," interrupted Mr Benton. "Just calm yourself down, and I'll come and have a look at it in a minute, when I've finished this meeting."

Mr Benton never rushed into things.

The carding engineer stumped out, tut-tutting as he went, as if to say, "I've more to do than wait for you to come down."

We finished our meeting.

"Keith, would you like to go down with me and see what you think about it?"

I readily agreed, wondering how he would deal with the situation.

When we got down to the carding room, the machine stood still and quiet like some lazy, overfed animal; the quietness in the room was almost tangible.

The carding engineer saw us, and came over to us. "Now, then, Mr Benton, just look at those tapes. It just isn't carding right."

"Just calm down a minute, Mr Carr. Let me have a look. Will you get me some spanners, please?" One of the machine workers turned to get the spanners. "And I shall need some feeler gauges."

A moment later, still dressed in his immaculate grey suit, and armed with spanners and feeler gauges, he clambered on to the machine at one end, studied the machinery carefully for a minute or so, then put the feeler gauge in.

With these machines the rollers have to be set at certain, precise distances, one to another, in order to get a good carding action. The skill, or craft, of the carding engineer is to know exactly what those distances are, and to be able to make the appropriate adjustments.

Bearing in mind that this engineer had been an apprentice and had been through the mill, and was still finding difficulty sorting out this machine for this particular batch of wool, Graham Benton had a job on his hands this time.

He slackened off one nut, put the feeler gauge in, tightened it up, slackened another nut, tightened it, moved on down the machine, slackening off, gauging, tightening up, right to the end of the machine.

Eventually, he gingerly came down from the machine, turned to the engineer, and said, "Now, Mr Carr, start her up, and see if that's done the trick."

The lazy, overfed animal woke, and began to puff; it ran as smoothly and as gracefully as a panther, and carded absolutely spot on. It was just right. We three stood for a while, looking and listening – no overfed, lazy animal now.

"You'll be alright now, Mr Carr. See you later. Come on, Keith. Let's have another look at that blend of wool we were looking at earlier."

No fuss, no big deal made of it; the whole thing was quite natural to him. It was then that I began to realise that this man knew his job. He'd been brought up in the mill, had spent long hours on the factory floor, and had never lost his skill – he knew the machines as well as he knew the business of running a mill. There are not so many people in his position who could do this, and I couldn't fail to be impressed.

It wasn't an easy job that I'd come into; there was still a lot to learn. I'd been at Benton's probably about a month when a strange incident took place. It is as clear in my mind today as it was then.

I'd pulled up in the outside lane at traffic lights one morning, as I was on my way to work. A car, a Jaguar, pulled up alongside my car, and, out of the corner of my eye, I became aware of the driver of the Jaguar attracting my attention. I recognised immediately the cheerful face of Brian Porter, my old boss from so many years ago. I hadn't seen him for years. He looked thinner than I remembered him, and quite pale.

"How's the new job going?" he shouted across, as I wound the passenger window down.

"It's great, Brian!" I shouted back. "I'm enjoying every minute of it."

"Jolly good!" And he waved as he sped away, as the lights changed to green.

I owed Brian Porter a lot. He was the one who had set me on my way, had helped me to understand what the wool industry was all about – all those years ago. Brian had seemed to me quite elderly even then, but I do not think it an exaggeration to say that we respected each other very much, and, in a way, became firm friends.

As I drove along, I became aware of the years that had rolled by – where had they all gone? – and how I, too, was beginning to feel the weight of years. And even just the previous month, Brian must have helped me obtain this job. It came to me like a hammer blow that I had failed to thank him for all he had done for me. That was inexcusable. I resolved to try to contact him that day.

I tried unsuccessfully to reach him on the phone; there was no answer. I tried again on several occasions over the following days. Eventually, I came to the conclusion he must have gone on holiday.

Less than a week later after our brief meeting, Graham called me into his office. He looked very serious when he asked me to sit down.

"I'm sorry, Keith," he said, turning away from me to pour a cup of tea. "I'm afraid I've some bad news for you."

There was a pause and a silence, broken only by the rattle of a teacup on its saucer. He turned and slowly handed me the cup of tea.

"Brian Porter passed away last night."

Graham turned back to his pouring.

I gulped. I don't know what bad news I'd been expecting, but, whatever it was, it was not this.

I looked blankly out of the window, as it began to sink in. Brian had been fighting cancer for some time, but, somehow, his death was unexpected – death always is – and I hadn't been prepared for this calm pronouncement.

It's sometimes odd how the brain reacts to sudden shocks. As I was gazing into the far distance, trying to put a tongue to my thoughts to say how sorry I was to hear the news, it came to me that I'd not managed to contact Brian to thank him for all he'd done for me, especially in helping me obtain this position I was now beginning to enjoy so much.

I could feel tears beginning to burn my eyes, a deep sense of sadness weighing heavily on me.

I got up, turned away, and left the room without a word.

Back in my own office, I was left to think what I had lost. It would have been so simple to say, "Thanks, Brian," but the opportunity was gone, and I would never have the chance to put it right. It was so sad – I could never now tell him how much I appreciated all he'd done for me.

The memorial service that was held for him some time later packed our church. People from every branch of the textile industry came to pay their last respects to a man who epitomised everything that was good about the industry; he was a gentleman, and a gentle man; he understood both his job and people, and, though he was only middle-aged when he died, somehow his death seemed to symbolise the passing of an era.

Dear old Bill gave the address, and it must have been an awful day for him, now that he had lost his lifelong business partner. For me, too, that afternoon, I knew I had lost a good friend, and I recalled the experiences we'd shared in our working lives.

There was a strong image in my mind's eye of Brian's smiling face as he sped off from the traffic lights the last time I saw him.

"Very sad," said Graham, as we came out of church.

"It certainly is," I replied.

"Still, life's got to go on, you know."

Refuge in a time-worn cliché.

We stood together, my boss and myself, in silent contemplation for a while. We shared the loss of a mutual friend, and I began to be aware of a new rapport between us, that I was working for a man whom I respected, both as a boss and as a person. I knew I was going to find my niche here, and it was a comfortable feeling.

Though I'd been appointed as wool-buyer for the firm, Graham always took it upon himself to make the final decision as to whether we bought wool or not. I was happy to accept that it was his mill and his money, and if he wanted that final responsibility of how the money was spent, so be it.

Graham was typical of many mill-owners of the time. In many ways he was old-fashioned; he always greeted the wool men with, "I see the market's down again this morning." The market could be going up or down in leaps and bounds, but as far as he was concerned, it was always on the way down. That's the character of these old mill men – they know what the market's doing, but that's the way they talk.

They know, too, that they'll have to bargain hard for their price; even so, such is the game to be played by buyer and seller, if pence are to be haggled over to be taken off the price of wool, then, sure enough, they'll add pence to the price of the wool before the bargaining starts. It's a charade as old as the hills. And if Graham could get a penny off the price of wool, then he'd do his damnedest to get it.

I got to know a wool salesman called Tony very well. I remember him calling in on us one day.

"If you think Graham's a difficult customer, you should meet this chap over in Ireland; he beats the lot," Tony said.

"I don't believe it," I replied.

"It's true. There's a wool buyer at this small mill in Ireland. Chap called McMahon, and he's got to be seen to be believed. I went out there a couple of months ago, and I said to myself, come hell or high water, I'd make him buy some of our wool. It'd never happened before, but this time, whatever it took, this McMahon was going to buy our wool.

The night before I was due to go out there, I had a phone call from George Pratt – he's a wool salesman who used to work at Kennedy's. He'd heard that I was on my way out to see McMahon.

"Where are you staying?" he'd asked. I told him. "I'm staying there, too. Tell you what; whoever gets an order from McMahon, the other buys dinner that night. OK?" I readily agreed.

The following morning I arrived at the mill, and was greeted by McMahon. It must have been about eleven o'clock by this time. "Nice to see you again, Tony. Come in. How's the wool?" said McMahon, as we went into his office.

"Oh, not so good, Mr McMahon. In fact, prices are down, way down. There's never been a better time to buy," I replied. "New Zealand prices are the best price you can get for years ahead."

"What are your current prices?" he asked.

"£1.25 per kilo," I said.

"What? £1.25 per kilo? That's a bit steep," he said, with a shrug of his shoulders. "That won't do. I'll tell you something. I wasn't going to mention it, but I've just had a chap in here no more than an hour or so ago – you must have just missed him as you came in – from one of the other firms, and he was offering £1.15."

I thought, "The cheeky beggar; George's got in before me after all."

"£1.15, Mr McMahon?"

"That's right. £1.15. I bought quite a bit off him at that price. I might be tempted to get some more."

"Mr McMahon, I'm determined you'll buy some of our wool today. If I've got to come down to £1.15, so be it."

And with that, we clinched the deal for a container of wool. But I can tell you this; I was pretty cheesed off with the price it'd come down to.

"When I got back to my hotel," Tony continued, "I met George just as he was coming into the lounge.

"Well, George, you dropped me right in it this time."

"What do you mean?" asked George, looking puzzled. "It was you who dropped me in it," he said, with some bitterness. "I call that a bit sharp, if you ask me."

"Hang on a minute," I said. "It was your fault for dropping your price so far."

"Only because you'd dropped yours to £1.15 before I got there."

"No, I didn't. McMahon told me you'd already been and gone."

"What time did you see him?"

"Eleven o'clock."

"Eleven o'clock! He told me you'd been in at half past nine, and he'd bought from you at £1.15 a kilo."

"Well, as it happened, I was in at about eleven, and, thinking you'd offered £1.15, I dropped my price to £1.10 to get any order at all. It's hardly been worth the trip."

"The crafty old buzzard!" exclaimed George. "You can see what he's done – he's played us off against each other."

"And it was true," concluded Tony. "He'd well and truly got the better of us on this occasion."

I suppose you'd got to give credit to this Mr McMahon. He was in the business of buying in for his firm, and if, for once, he'd managed to shave a few pence off, it may be sharp practice, but he'd succeeded in getting it at a favourable price, one way or another.

In later years, I used to call there myself to sell him yarn, and it was always the same ploy that he'd use; he'd quote mythical figures from the mill down the road. Fortunately, being aware of his opening gambit, we always used to go prepared with inflated prices for our yarn. We, too, could play his game.

CHAPTER 10

Under Graham, as I said earlier, I did everything in the mill – well, almost every job. Apart from doing the costings and working out prices, I used to see quite a few of the customers, but, before long, a new avenue of responsibility opened up for me.

At our meetings, Graham and I used to discuss the reports submitted by our agents. A lot of our business was transacted through these agents, and we relied – and still do rely – on the business acumen and skill of our field agents.

"What do you think of this report?" Graham asked one day, tossing a rather thin report across the desk to me. I scanned it through, then took a closer look.

"Well, I think we can do better," I replied. "We don't seem to be getting the sort of business we might expect from this area."

"I agree. How about you going down there and chivvying him on a bit? You know the set up. You know what the market can do. What do you say? Go round with him, meet some of the customers – that sort of approach."

"It's something I've not done before, but I don't mind."

"Right, then, Keith. Take a couple of days next week, get yourself down to the Midlands, have a chat with him, then do a spot of touring round with him."

At the time, nearly all my work time was spent in the mill.

The prospect of getting out for a couple of days, staying at a hotel, working away from the mill, pleased me quite a lot.

The following week saw me back at Graham's office.

"How've you got on then, Keith?" Graham asked, as I walked in.

"Fine, Mr Benton. It's been really good. I've enjoyed it."

"To be honest, Keith, I've had a few words with some of the customers you met..."

I thought, "The crafty beggar. He's been checking on me, as well."

"They all appear very impressed with you. I'm glad you enjoyed the trip."

A couple of weeks later, he came into my office.

"Right, I shan't be here for the next few days. Will you hold the fort for me? I'm going to see a couple of our customers in Denmark."

By this time, I was quite used to 'holding the fort' – this was nothing new to me. Sure enough, he was back in three days. He looked tired and drawn.

"I'm getting a bit old for all this travel. It's getting too much for me now," was his only comment.

Nothing more was said about it. Then about six weeks after this Denmark trip, I happened to be in his office when he took a phone call from our Scandinavian agent – a very industrious, quietly assured and highly competent agent called Fredrik. I'd met him on three or four occasions when he'd come over to visit the mill. He liked to see for himself how things were progressing.

For some reason, Fredrik was unable to pay his customary visit this year.

"Not to worry," I heard Graham say. "I'll pop over to you for a change, and we can perhaps see a few customers. Or, better still," he added, looking straight at me, "I'll send Keith over. OK?"

He put the phone down.

"Fancy going?"

"Well, er, I don't know. I don't speak..."

"Nor do I. They all speak English. You'll enjoy it. They're very pleasant people over there, our customers."

And that was it – the decision had been made. I was to go to Denmark and Sweden. You might just have told me that I was going to go to the moon – the distance was about the same. I hadn't even got a passport.

A few weeks later, I was being driven to Manchester Airport and I was extremely nervous, and I remember sitting in the car, clutching my new passport, wondering how everything would turn out in the next few days. It was early November, and the plane that would take me from Manchester to Copenhagen was shrouded in mist, as it stood on the runway.

I'd got my yarn samples in my bag, and my head was swimming with figures of costings. I could still hear Graham's final instructions ringing in my ears, "Keith, whatever you do, you can't afford to waffle. Give them straight answers, if they ask. Don't let them think you don't know what you're talking about. You need to be clear in your own mind what approach to take, and what will go. Alright?"

I'd said I was alright but the truth was some way away.

Fredrik was waiting for me with his car when we reached Copenhagen at about nine in the evening.

We exchanged greetings, and soon we were on our way.

"We're heading for Sweden," he said.

"When?" I asked.

"Tonight. We should be there, via Helsingor and car ferry, by midnight, all being well."

He spoke English well, with only a trace of accent. It was quite pleasing to the ear. "I have arranged for you to meet our first Swedish customers at ten tomorrow morning. We must make sure we are there on time."

"Naturally," I replied, with nagging apprehension increasing all the time.

Just over three hours later, we reached our hotel. The journey had sped by, as Fredrik filled me in with as much background as possible. He was a good agent and certainly knew both his job and our customers thoroughly.

After a good night's rest, we set off again, this time to our first customers. The mill was situated about forty or so kilometres from Gothenburg. It was a large mill and well set up.

"They are excellent carpet manufacturers," said Fredrik, "but we've not had a lot of business from them in the past. We really need to get something going here, if we can. It will be a good market for our firm."

I was, understandably, quite nervous as we entered the mill yard. Soon we were shown to the M.D.'s office, and were introduced to Mr Nielsen, the managing director, and a young-looking, fair-haired assistant called Christoff.

"Tell me a little about your company," said Mr Nielsen, after he had outlined a brief history of his own company.

I went through all the rigmarole of recounting who and what we were – a part I'd rehearsed quite a number of times before. I knew it so well that it felt almost as if I was speaking the part of a stage character.

"Well," he said at length, "we might be very interested in purchasing from your company, depending on price, of course. We should like 80/20 wool nylon at 3.5 metric. Does that present any problems?"

He could see the worried look on my face.

"Er, no, Mr Nielsen. No problems at all." Except that I had worked out all my calculations at 3.25 metric.

"You can give me a price for this, yes?"

"Certainly. I've got all the prices worked out with the wool dyed," I said, trying to sound confident.

"I would like the price, please, with the wool not dyed. Thank you. I would like it in oil."

"Oh, crikey!" I muttered to myself. I reached for my calculator and began to convert the prices. My fingers tapped feverishly on the calculator, and my mind was a whirl of figures.

"There is no rush, Mr Haigh. Please take your time."

He turned to gaze out of the window. All the time, Christoff sat unsmiling, deep in contemplation, at the side of the desk, and I could feel his curious gaze directed on to the page of my calculations.

A couple of minutes later – it seemed a great deal longer – I had the calculations done.

"Er... er... £2.65," I blurted out. "£2.65, Mr Nielsen."

"One moment, please."

He opened a book on his desk, speaking quietly to Christoff, as he did so. I should have liked to know what he was saying at that precise moment. I could almost have imagined him saying something like, "Well, we've a real idiot here, quoting this sort of price. There's money to be made out of this deal if we play our cards right." I still felt very nervous, and figures kept coming into my mind. I was only too aware that this was my first attempt to do a deal on my own with a customer, and I felt my inexperience was showing, like a hole in a sock.

At that moment, after a quick glance at Christoff, who nodded slightly back to him, Mr Nielsen turned to me.

"I think that sounds a very fair price, Mr Haigh," he said, smiling as he said it. "We wish to order sixty tonnes.

The best I could do was a blank sort of stare.

"Sixty tonnes?"

Maybe I'd misheard.

"Sixty tonnes," he affirmed. "Is that alright?"

"Er, yes, I'm sure it will be."

"Good. Then that is settled." He stood up, and we shook hands.

I was in a state of something near shock, as I entered the order in my book. I couldn't wait to get out to check my figures and see where I'd gone wrong.

The office door closed behind us as Fredrik and I made our way back to the car. He didn't speak as we walked. All the time I was trying to work out where I'd gone wrong with my calculations. It was the sack for me, no doubt about it.

"Well," said Fredrik, unhelpfully, as we sat in the car, "you're the one who knows the prices. I cannot help you in this matter."

That was correct, of course. This wasn't Fredrik's responsibility. I was the one who had to take the blame.

I noticed Fredrik's car phone.

"Get Graham on the phone for me, will you, please." I might as well know the worst now as later.

After what seemed an age, Graham came on the phone. He sounded very cheerful.

"Now, then, Keith, how're you getting on?" he asked. "Are you getting any orders for us?"

"How about sixty tonnes?"

There was silence on the other end of the line.

"Pardon?"

"How about sixty tonnes?"

"How about them?"

"Well, that's what I've got."

"Don't be so daft. Sixty tonnes?"

"Yes; sixty tonnes to be delivered over three months at £2.65.

"How did you get your price?"

"I worked it out whilst I was there."

I thought I heard what sounded like a groan.

"I've got to go now. Must check that figure. Bye."

And with that he was gone.

I died a thousand deaths during the rest of that trip, and a condemned murderer could not have endured more troubled sleep.

The following Monday, I walked into the mill, feeling very apprehensive. "Let's get it over with," I thought.

Graham met me at the door

"Welcome back!" he beamed. "That was quite a decent price you got over there. You've done well! Come to my office and we'll have a cup of coffee whilst we talk."

And that was all there was to it, and I'd believed I'd be on my way back home by now. So confident was I of this that I'd given Philippa instructions to have a coffee ready for me in about half an hour!

Well, that took place some years ago now, and experience has taught me a lot of things. I don't say I know all the answers even now, but, as you get older, you somehow keep things in better proportion, and you're better aware of your situation.

Still, you can always meet the totally unexpected, and you can still be thrown off your guard, no matter how experienced you are. It all depends. Suffice to say, from that day to this, I've never booked sixty tonnes as easily as that, and it's still a mystery to me how I did it.

As a sort of postscript to that episode, that inexperienced young man, Christoff, who sat alongside the managing director's table at that meeting, worked his way up through the ranks to become general manager himself, and it has been my pleasure to meet him on numerous occasions since that first encounter. You couldn't hope to meet a more charming and businesslike gentleman.

That, briefly, was how I came to be launched on a sales career, a totally new and unexpected twist in my career, but not unwelcome, for all that.

Not so long after that first, memorable, Scandinavian trip, I found myself back there again in a small town in the south of Denmark. It was the centre of the textile industry in Denmark, and was producing excellent quality goods for the world market.

Fredrik and I were once again teamed up to meet at a particular mill on the outskirts of the town. When we arrived, the contrast with the setting of some of our own mills in England could not have been more acute. Beautifully laid out and manicured gardens, colourful and bright with flowers, surrounded modern, attractive buildings. If you must work in a mill, it must be most pleasant to work in a place like this. (It is only in recent years, as I write, that there has been a concerted effort to make industrial premises here in the north more 'environmentally friendly'. And what a difference that has made. Some of the old rundown industrial areas have been improved beyond all recognition – but not before time.)

Two young ladies greeted us at the door, showed us to the boardroom, there to be met by a young man who warmly welcomed us and made us feel at ease.

Coffee and pastries were served, and I couldn't help thinking that this was the way business should be conducted. It was civil, charming, and very welcome.

Hans, the young man, explained there had been a slight problem in the mill. Fredrik asked if I minded if he and Hans went down into the mill to see what the problem was, which would give me a little time to work out some more figures for prices that Hans had asked for.

As I sat there working out the prices, I could feel that I was being watched through the half-open door of the boardroom. Looking up, I could see a little man standing there, dressed in brown boots and a shabby, khaki-coloured coat reaching nearly down to his boots. He seemed to be peering at me over the top of bottle-glass lenses. When he saw me looking at him, he smiled and nodded, so I smiled and nodded back to him. "Must be one of the cleaning staff," I thought. He disappeared, and in a minute or two came back again. Again he smiled and nodded, and I did the same. It was becoming quite amusing. He seemed a very amiable chap.

Fredrik and Hans returned, and sat down at the table. To my surprise, the little man shuffled in after them, and sat down alongside Hans, and again nodded and smiled. I was quite used to this procedure by now. Nobody else seemed to take any notice of him, so I, too, ignored him, after I had given him the statutory nod and smile.

Our meeting was cordial and efficient; every now and again Hans would say something in the general direction of the little man, who would nod and smile at him, then nod and smile at us. It was quite touching, and quite comical. When lunch was served – they really know how to look after their guests – the little man declined to join us, but promptly dived under the table to retrieve a plastic lunch box. Having opened it up, he carefully undid cellophane-wrapped sandwiches, and munched at these with gusto.

After the meeting, we shook hands, including the little man, who nodded and smiled, nodded and smiled, until we were out and nearly back to the car.

"Who the heck was that!" I spluttered, having contained my amusement for so long. "He's the funniest little bloke I've seen for ages, Who the heck was he? Have you ever met him before?" I asked Fredrik.

"Well, as a matter of fact, I have met him before. He's a very pleasant chap." He paused for a moment. "He's the owner of the firm."

"No!"

"Yes, he is; he always comes to the meetings, but doesn't speak a word of English - always leaves negotiations to his son, Hans. Never been anywhere more than ten miles from the mill, Hans tells me, and always wears that shabby coat. He's not changed in twenty or more years."

"Well, who would've believed it!" I replied, still trying to work out how an odd little chap like that could have built up an enterprise as big and efficient as the one we'd just seen. You can't always judge people by first appearances.

Since those early days, I've travelled a great deal – not always, I might add, to exotic places. On one occasion, I received a phone call from London one Friday afternoon. A man speaking in very broken English introduced himself as a meat trader, but he had been told to contact me. I couldn't work out how and why a meat trader had been told to contact me. That was just the first of a number of odd circumstances.

"There is a delegation coming to London tomorrow from the Middle East," he said. "They wish to discuss the yarn which your firm has. They wish you, please, to be in London tomorrow morning at 11.00 a.m. at the Marble Arch Hotel. You understand?"

I understood alright, but it all sounded a bit peculiar.

Graham, who had heard most of the conversation, nodded approval. "You will carry a rolled up newspaper under your arm, and be in the reception area tomorrow at 11 a.m."

I agreed, but still wondered what I was letting myself in for.

The following morning, I caught the early train, and, as instructed, was in the hotel with my rolled up newspaper in reception, feeling a bit stupid and thinking this was all some silly game.

"Mr Haigh?"

The sound came out from the back of the throat, as if he were clearing phlegm from it.

"Yes."

I turned to see two very well-dressed gentlemen standing there. Unfamiliar with Mediterranean distinctions, I thought they could have come from any of the countries round that region.

"We wish to discuss your yarn. Please follow us."

They led me into a small room at the back of the hotel. We went in and sat down. I was sitting facing these two dark-skinned men whose names, even, I did not know.

"Proceed, please."

For the next ten minutes or so, I gave them details of our organisation and production, and all the while they sat impassively staring back at me. I'd no idea whether I was making sense to them or not. It was quite weird.

When I'd finished, one of them spoke.

"Abdul" – of all names it had to be Abdul! – "Abdul will take you to see the Major General. The Major General is in charge of this buying expedition, and you will meet him at our Embassy.

"When you go, you will be shown into a room with the Major General. You will only speak when he speaks, and you will not sit if he is standing, and only sit down when he invites you to do so. You understand?"

I told him I understood, though I could feel my hackles rising, as he continued to patronise me. It was beginning to feel even more like some film or other, as if James Bond was going to appear at any moment.

We drove in a magnificent limousine to the Embassy. When we arrived, Abdul took me to a room, opened the door, and introduced me, as we went in, to a man dressed in civilian clothes.

First impressions again gave me the notion that he looked distinctly shabby. I'd expected something rather better.

During the next two hours, we went through all our prices and I told him what we were able to do. He told me he was interested in government contracts. His questions were very searching, and he certainly knew the business.

At the end of the meeting, I was ushered out of the room, after making a little bow to him, and was shepherded back to the hotel in the same limousine in which I'd arrived.

Abdul, who had hardly spoken a word, said to me, "Did you enjoy your meeting with the Major General?"

"Yes," I replied, "it was quite an amicable meeting."

"Good. You have agreed prices, yes?"

I told him we had.

"Very good. We now need to make special arrangements. You will invoice this to our government, but you will add 15% to your prices. This 15% will be sent to the hotel where the Major General is staying. You understand?"

"We'll be waiting at the hotel until Monday morning for your answer. Goodbye, Mr Haigh."

And with that they were gone.

When I got back, I told the whole story to Graham, his eyes growing wider and wider with amazement as the story unfolded. The more I talked, the whiter he became.

"Get that Abdul on the phone!" he said, with some degree of urgency in his voice, as I finished my account.

I rang the number I'd been given. After a while, the same voice I'd listened to a few days ago came over the phone.

"Listen!" said Graham. "I don't do business with people like you. We do business straight, you understand? You'll have to go and buy your yarn somewhere else." And promptly banged the phone down.

And that was the end of that. I suppose Abdul would have just shrugged his shoulders, and set up a deal somewhere else together with the 15%. But, even so, I admired Graham for his one-man stand against what he considered to be a corrupt way of trading. It didn't do for him, and he wasn't having any of it, though we lost quite a sizeable order on that occasion.

CHAPTER 11

Every new job throws up new situations and new challenges. This was particularly the case in my early days at Benton's.

I was sitting in my office one day, when there was a knock at the door, and in walked a young Afro-Caribbean woman. I'd seen her about the mill, but I didn't really know her too well. She sat down and introduced herself. Her name was Pearl Jackson. She said she had a complaint to make: that she was a victim of racial discrimination.

"Well, that surprises me," I replied, for I was pretty sure that all employees at Benton's got fair and equitable treatment. You'd better tell me about it."

"There's a woman who works in the end office, in the wages section," Pearl began. "Every time I leave the mill at the end of my shift, she looks at me funny. She watches me. I don't like her staring at me. It is because of my colour."

"I see. How long has this been going on?"

"For the past two weeks. When I go home in the evening, I pass her office window. She stares at me."

She was very earnest and looked very upset.

"We'd better try and sort this thing out straightaway, then," I said. "You say that one of our employees deliberately stares at you."

"That is right. I think her name is Carol, but I am not sure."

"And have you spoken to her about it?"

"No; I do not like her."

"But, surely, if you spoke with her, you might find there's nothing in it."

"She is like all the others in this mill. They do not like us because we are coloured."

I could see that here was a problem. We had now moved, so to speak, from one worm to the whole can of worms. On first hearing, I didn't think her comments were reasonable; Benton's had an excellent record of fair play for all. Nevertheless, there could easily be incidents and personal differences.

"Hang on a minute, Mrs Jackson. Let's stick to one thing at a time. I'll go and talk to this Carol. Just give me a few minutes."

I left my office and strode along to the wages section, walked in, and approached the girl whom Mrs Jackson had accused.

"Carol," I said, "do you know a woman called Pearl, Pearl Jackson, down on the shop floor?"

"I've seen her around," she replied, "but I've not spoken to her, not that I know of."

"I've received a complaint from her. She says that you stare at her when she passes your office window here."

Carol looked at me blankly. She hadn't a clue what I was talking about. I knew Carol reasonably well, and couldn't imagine that she would deliberately be offensive to anyone.

"Well, I'm sorry, Mr Haigh," she said, her face reddening. "That's simply not true. I can't even think I've ever seen her leaving the mill. Besides, I don't make a habit of 'looking funny' at people. If I've any problems with people, I tell them to their face."

"And you've never had any words with this person?"

"No; but I feel like having a few words with her now."

"Not to worry, Carol. I'm sure there's been some mistake. I'll see if I can sort this out."

I went back to my office.

"Pearl, I've spoken with this girl, er... Carol. She tells me that what you say is completely untrue, and she hardly even knows you."

Mrs Jackson stood up, turned and said something I didn't catch, as she stormed out of my office, slamming the door so hard that a file of papers on a cabinet nearby fluttered to the floor.

A fortnight after this uncomfortable interview with Mrs Jackson, I received a letter. It was from the Race Relations Board, as I knew it then, informing us of a complaint they'd received from one of our workers, concerning racial harassment. The matter was to be investigated.

I was horrified and couldn't believe it. I immediately took the letter in to show Mr Benton.

"Tell me the whole story," he said, quietly.

I related the incident to him from the beginning. He listened in silence. Knowing him, I thought he'd tell them to take a running jump into the lake - he didn't usually have time for these kind of people. When I'd finished, he thought for a while.

"Tell them to come and see us. Make an appointment for them, and let's speak with them."

I was rather surprised by this decision, but I made the appointment, as requested.

Not so many days later, I was informed that there was a person from the Race Relations Board in reception. I introduced myself, the representative from Race Relations was a woman, slightly younger than myself, and dressed rather severely in tweed suit and lisle stockings.

"Mary Ledshaw. I've come to investigate the complaint the Board has received," she said.

"So I understand, Mrs Ledshaw."

"Ms."

"Sorry?"

"Ms."

"Ah, I see. Please come with me. Mr Benton wishes to speak with you himself "

"I should expect him to," she replied, a little self-importantly, I thought.

I took her up to the boardroom, ordered tea and informed Mr Benton that the representative from the Race Relations Board had arrived.

A couple of minutes later he came in.

"I'm here," she began, without much preamble, "to consider the complaint made against your firm by one of your employees, a Mrs Pearl Jackson. You are familiar with the details, I understand?"

"Well," replied Mr Benton, "Keith has given me the outline of it. How do you see the problem?"

"I understand that one of your employees, Miss Carol Dunning, has been subjecting Mrs Jackson to unwarrantable harassment. Mrs Jackson has said that she believes the problem to be racially motivated.

"It is a serious complaint, Mr Benton, and one we at the Race Relations Board don't treat lightly. We don't condone this sort of thing. We shall never make progress until we start to deal with all employees in a fair, equitable and suitable manner."

"I couldn't agree with you more," Mr Benton replied.

She then went on to relate the problem as it had been passed to her, stressing that the firm had a responsibility in this matter, and alleging that Benton's had done nothing to help either her, or any of the coloured people working in the mill.

Mr Benton listened, and looked very concerned.

"So, Mr Benton," she said, finally, "what do you intend to do about it? What policy does your firm adopt on such an issue?"

Mr Benton looked at her carefully, then turned to me.

"Keith," he said, "I think, rather than answer this immediately, we'd better let this lady talk to our senior foreman in charge."

"I think you're missing the point," she began. "I can't see what relevance this foreman has. I would like to know what your policy is towards coloured people, or whether this matter should be taken further."

I could see she was irritated by having to talk to one of the shop floor workers.

"I assure you, Mrs Ledshaw..."

"Ms."

"Yes; if there are any major problems of this kind going on, our foreman will have a better view of the situation than I have. And I think we'd better have Mrs Jackson in as well."

I sent for them to come to the boardroom.

A couple of minutes later, Mrs Jackson walked in, and looked at each of us in turn. She sat down, and smiled at Ms Ledshaw.

"Our foreman won't be long now," said Graham. "Despite what you seem to be saying, Ms Ledshaw, we do try in this company to give all our employees an equal chance, and to ensure that instances of racial intolerance are seriously dealt with. That is our policy."

"Well, I'm sorry, Mr Benton. From what Mrs Jackson tells me, there appears little evidence of that."

There was a knock on the door.

" Ah, come in. Have a seat."

A young man, probably about twenty-six or twenty-seven entered. He was tall and slim, and you could imagine he could be a good athlete. He fixed his gaze on Mr Benton, as he walked in.

"Ms Ledshaw, I should like to introduce to you our winding and twisting foreman. He's been with us a few years now, and I've a lot of time for him. He'll know what's going on in the mill.

"Asif, this lady has come to investigate a complaint about racial harassment. Would you think there was a lot of this going on in the mill? Tell us if, and how, it has affected you."

Asif looked Ms Ledshaw straight in the eye. She sat there, pen poised to record it all.

"I left secondary modern school with no qualifications. Mr Benton paid for my college education, all my books and all my expenses. I enjoy working here very much. I have no problems with other work people. Most of us get on well here."

"You know Mrs Jackson. Can you tell me, please, why she is having all these problems?" asked Ms Ledshaw.

"To tell truth, I can't be doing with her. She just makes trouble all the time. She makes trouble for the other workers, too. Ask any of the workers. They, too, have had enough of her."

"That is not true. Asif is always picking on me."

"Do you 'pick on' Mrs Jackson, Asif?"

"I have a responsibility to all the workers on the shop floor. Mrs Jackson takes a lot of time off. No reason. She often arrives late, and has been many times warned. Last week, she said I was looking funny at her."

"You? She said you were looking funny at her?"

"Yes."

There was a pause.

Ms Ledshaw looked at Asif, then Mrs Jackson, then Graham Benton. She put her pen back in her handbag, and stood up.

"Thank you for your time, Mr Benton. I don't think I need detain you. There will be no need to take this matter any further. May I have a word with you, Mrs Jackson, before I leave?"

Two weeks later, Mrs Jackson handed in her notice. We were not sorry to see her go. Race relations are such fragile things; we didn't want anyone deliberately setting out to wreck what had been achieved at Benton's.

No company is perfect, but if the policy is to try to ensure that all workers can work without fear of harassment, or discrimination, then it's on the right road towards good working conditions. Hopefully! But that was just one occasion when I was glad of Graham Benton's assistance in handling what might, otherwise, have been an even more unpleasant situation.

CHAPTER 12

As my work in sales expanded, we used to show our yarns at various exhibitions up and down the country, and it was at the Wooltek Exhibition that I first met Colin Dyke.

From the beginning, we seemed to get on well together, mainly because we shared one particular grievance; at these exhibitions, we always felt that our firms were being pushed to the back of the queue, that French and Italian firms always seemed to receive a great deal more attention than we did from the agents. These agents were important to the firms, and, laughingly, we used to like to think that they were paid more commission from the continental firms than their British counterparts. In truth, I don't know whether they were or not. Perhaps, the continental firms gave them more business because they were better organised than we were.

Nevertheless, it was extremely irritating to play second fiddle, and more than one of these continental representatives seemed to go out of their way to try to make us feel inferior.

Colin, I should explain, was a cotton spinner from Lancashire. He was a Lancastrian through and through, with an accent as broad as Morecambe Bay. His manner was blunt, he spoke his mind, and you always knew where you stood with him. Perhaps the best thing about knowing Colin was his bluff, straight-faced humour, that sometimes cloaked itself in mock belligerence. He'd say to me, for example, when we were helping put up a display, "Pass me a hammer, Keith... Hammer... Do you have hammers in Yorkshire? Oh, I can't do with these people from Yorkshire. They're a queer lot over there. Thank heavens we don't have to meet them every day... You know what a hammer looks like, don't you..." And he'd keep up this banter continually.

I got to know him well and he was always good company, always striving to be the centre of attention, always wanting to be known and to know who he was dealing with.

Apart from anything else, he was exceptionally good at his job, and nothing he did or said altered his approach – you could never mistake him for anything but a dyed-in-the-wool Lancastrian; even when he was meeting VIPs from France or Germany, or wherever, they all got the same treatment. Professional and well-organised in all his work, he nevertheless never put on 'airs and graces' for anyone. He was what he was – and proud of it.

There was one particular occasion at the Wooltek Exhibition, when both Colin and I felt left out in the cold. The French and the Italians had done a really good job, but we seemed to be making little headway. The agents hardly had time for us.

One evening during the Exhibition, it was decided that there should be a leaving dinner for one of these agents at a local restaurant, to which Colin and I were invited.

When we arrived, the only places not taken were at opposite ends of a table occupied by two Frenchmen, two Italians, one German and one Dutchman. I do not think it was our imagination that caused us to feel out of it, in the presence of these continentals. From the start, their conversation turned to domestic matters which excluded both Colin and myself. Normally, we could both get on well with representatives from other countries – but not this time. Once again, we didn't feel part of the group, as they hogged the table talk. I caught a glimpse of Colin; he was sitting in silence, as isolated as I was.

It was Colin, as usual, who started it. On our previous meetings, the old Yorkshire – Lancashire quarrels had raised their heads in friendly rivalry. Today was going to be no exception; if we couldn't get along with these gentlemen at table, we'd provide our own entertainment.

"It's a right shame they built the M62, " said Colin, across the table. "There's far too many blummin' Yorkshire yobs comin' across t'Pennines. They should stay on their own side, and stop causin' bother."

The accent was deliberately exaggerated.

The gauntlet was down. One or two of the others looked at Colin, slightly puzzled. They weren't sure how to respond.

"Nay, lad," I said, "you're totally wrong there, as usual. The only time you tripe guzzlers ever get a bit of civilisation is when you meet us Yorkshire folk. You'd be still painting yourselves with woad, if people hadn't come across from our side."

Our continental acquaintances looked at me now, equally puzzled.

"Don't try to be funny!" exclaimed Colin. "Your only culture in Yorkshire is in't rhubarb sheds, and there in't much o'that nowadays."

There was silence from the others. Their knowledge of English was good enough to understand that 'something was going on'. As the banter came back and forth from each end of the table, their heads were turning like Wimbledon spectators.

"Well, what you've just said is a load of rhubarb, if you ask me," I replied.

"Who'd ask you?" said Colin, warming to the fun. "You Tykes are all the same. Just because you're born in Yorkshire, you all think you're something special. You've had to change your rule about playing for Yorkshire at cricket, though, haven't you, seeing that you've not won anything for the past twenty years."

"I'd rather lose with Yorkshire than win with Lancashire any time. And, anyway, half the Lancashire side are from abroad. Can't you find any decent players of your own?"

" 'Course we can. And we can win championships. Where were Leeds United last year, then? They're not in the same class as ManU."

It was the sort of verbal exchange we'd known since we'd been kids, and about the same intellectual level. Never mind, by this time, we were thoroughly enjoying ourselves, but I could see some consternation on the faces of the others at table. For the first time, we were not being ignored.

Speeches interrupted our exchanges, as we all wished a happy retirement to the representative. Having drunk a toast to him, we broke up into small groups, and Colin and I were all set to begin again.

One of the two French agents approached me.

"I am sorry," he said, "that you do not get on well with your British colleague. You must find it very difficult to work alongside him."

I couldn't help laughing.

"On the contrary," I said. "The sort of comments you may have just heard have been going on for years. Whenever we get together, Colin and myself fight the 'Wars of the Roses' all over again. It's a game we've played for ages; most people in Yorkshire and Lancashire understand what it's all about. It's just a bit of harmless fun when Yorkshire and Lancashire people meet. A bit of friendly rivalry."

"Then what you were saying at table was not meant to be taken serious?"

"Not at all! We're the best of friends, and we enjoy each other's company."

"Ah," said the Frenchman, with a shake of his head. "Many times I do not understand your British sense of humour. Perhaps I never will."

Very probably. Maybe there are things in Europe, after all, that can't be reached by Brussels' legislation. So much the better.

After that occasion, we didn't build any further international bridges, and the entente cordiale remained, for us, on ice.

The Wooltek Exhibition gave way, we were pleased to note, to the British Wool Exhibition, with only British firms represented. It was with the introduction of this new format Exhibition that, segregated from our continental rivals, we began to make real headway with our own businesses, and our order books began to fill up.

When the home market picked up, it was not long before there was more pressure to go further afield. 'PARYEX' beckoned – the International Paris Yarn Exhibition was too important to ignore.

"What do you reckon, Keith?" Colin asked me. "I've never been to Paris. I've always fancied going there."

"Sounds a good idea to me. I think it's time we extended into the Common Market. If the French and Italians can come over to us, it's time we reversed the process."

We soon talked our respective bosses into supporting our scheme. The plan was quite simple: fly to Paris Monday; see the Exhibition Tuesday, Wednesday and Thursday; make out our reports on the viability of our firms exhibiting the following year; fly home Thursday evening. It sounded a good plan.

In order to exhibit, we needed a competent designer for the display. Colin had a contact in Bootle, a young man called Alan, who was making a name for himself running his own design firm. He was only too pleased to come with us, and eager to impress.

Thus, the three of us landed in Paris one afternoon in early April. Spring sunshine made the city glow with its warmth.

Whatever anyone has ever written, or sung, about April in Paris, we knew then what that feeling was – of being in the most beautiful city in the world, and seeing it coming to life again, after the winter, in a blaze of colour – it is almost indescribable, the feeling of warmth, and friendliness, and sheer pleasure of being there.

Above all, it's true what they say; when you're in Paris, you feel young. It's a city of youth, unmistakably – a little bit like being in a university or college town in England, only on a much grander scale.

By contrast, I hadn't been on top form myself for quite some time, feeling tired and listless. I couldn't put my finger on it, but, somehow, I had a feeling, even then, that things were going to get worse – much worse – before there was any chance of them getting better. What was wrong, I just didn't suspect, at the time, despite the previous warnings I'd had when I was at Walter Standish's.

However, here, in Paris, I began to feel again some of the joy of life – and the vitality to go with it.

The flowering cherry trees were a profusion of delicate pink blossom all along the Tuileries Gardens; we dashed across the frantic Place de la Concorde – don't ever complain to me about the standard of driving in this country! We strolled up the Champs-Élysees to the Arc de Triomphe. On that spring afternoon, we were a million miles from the mills of England. It was pure joy.

There, on the Champs-Élysees, we did what generations of tourists have done; we sat at a table outside one of the many cafés for a while, not only drinking the wildly expensive coffee, but drinking in the unique atmosphere of Paris, the Paris of perfume and garlic, of little gendarmes, of tiny tots jabbering away in fluent French, of bouquinistes, cars driven on to the pavements, and that vast moving army of tourists, coming into the city to celebrate Easter.

Hundreds, if not thousands, of visitors and Parisians, were sitting, like us, at other cafés, and waiters flitted in and out, like butterflies, to attend to their customers. Even as they served one group at one table, their eyes darted back and forth to catch the glances of those still waiting to be served.

Colin hadn't been to Paris before; I'd been on two other, albeit brief, occasions before, and Alan knew the place, he thought, quite well. Even so, though I liked to impress Colin with my worldly wisdom – it was a long-running joke with us – I left it to Alan to lead the way, and show us around.

Our hotel was just off George V Avenue, so we hadn't far to walk from the Champs-Élysees.

"What I'd like," said Colin, "is a really good French dinner. You know, the sort of dinner that'll give me a right good idea about this

French cuisine. Then I'll know what France is all about. I'm really looking forward to it."

Alan and I agreed that we would give Colin an evening in Paris that he wouldn't forget. How right we were!

It was decided that Alan would guide us to the Latin Quarter in the evening for us to enjoy a typical French meal.

From the moment we set out, the evening was a shambles. Alan led us to the Métro, chose the route, but where we emerged was anybody's guess – probably as far away from the Latin Quarter as when we set out.

He tried again; it was simple enough, but again we were lost. By the time we found ourselves in the Latin Quarter, it would have been much easier to walk there. Colin's feet were sore, we were all fed up, and we were seriously hungry. In his inimitable fashion, Colin had a few choice (Lancashire) epithets to describe Alan and myself (though I didn't know why I was to blame), and Paris, and the whole disastrous evening.

"The next bistro we come to," I said, with some determination, as we plodded along Rue Saint Michel, "is where we shall eat."

They agreed.

We turned a corner, the tables were set out on the pavement – that was the place where we would eat. We decided to go inside, and we sat down at a table. It was only when we'd ordered a preliminary drink that we realised that Colin wouldn't get his typical French dinner that he'd looked forward to for so long – not in this restaurant, anyway – we were in a Greek restaurant!

"Waiter!" Colin beckoned the waiter to him. "Isn't that just typical of Yorkshire people? They say they're going to take you out for a typical French meal…" The waiter stood by, looking at Colin, with absolutely no comprehension. "…and where do you think they bring me? They bring me to a Greek restaurant! Now what do you think of that, then? We've a name for people like that, where I come from. What do you think of them, eh?"

All the while, the waiter's gaze shifted from Colin, to me, then to Alan. He smiled, but he hadn't a clue what Colin was getting at. My 'O' Level French (failed) wasn't much good either, and, eventually, he shrugged his shoulders, pointed at the menu, and proceeded to take our orders.

What with the tedious travel round the Métro, his aching feet, the disappointment of the meal, Colin left Alan and me in no doubt that he wasn't best pleased with the way the evening had gone!

After the meal – enjoyable of its kind, but not what Colin had wanted – we eventually made our way back to our hotel, where, miraculously, he produced a bottle of brandy, which we all enjoyed. It rounded off the evening better than we had hoped – or, some of it, at least. Not having eaten very much, Colin was much the worse for the brandy, and it took a couple of turns round the Arc de Triomphe to bring him round, sufficiently for him to go to bed to sleep! He regretted his excesses the following morning.

The rest of our time in Paris however, fulfilled our wildest expectations. In between visiting the Yarn Exhibition, we found time to sample some of the pleasures of this great city.

From Notre-Dame to the Eiffel Tower, and from Montmartre to the bateaux-mouches on the Seine, we made the most of our brief sojourn. Colin, as always, was good company, and Alan fitted in extremely well. There is so much to see in Paris that, even in a month of Sundays, you'd still be bewildered by its attractions. And the thing I've most noted about Paris: you don't really need actually to go anywhere – wherever you are, whether on the banks of the river, by the Opera, out at Versailles, or wherever, you can just simply sit and take in a whole new world. The people themselves are an endless source of interest.

Not least of these attractions are the women who pass you in the street. So many women, so stylish in appearance, so elegant; they're a pleasure simply to look at, and admire.

Dark hair, olive complexion, and dark eyes are a lethally seductive cocktail; there's something rather special about seeing a young woman striding confidently along the Rue de Rivoli.

A gentle stroll round the Galeries Lafayette gave us, indeed, much to admire. 'Les Parisiennes' seem to know instinctively how to present themselves attractively, and to make the most of themselves – an observation that Colin furnished us with from time to time, obviously becoming quite a connoisseur on the subject.

It is a pity, though, that these most attractive French ladies eat garlic! That is why most of them, as far as I am concerned, are seen at their best at a distance. Encounter one, face to face in the Métro, and you know that garlic should be banned for ever.

Thursday came too soon – far too soon – there was still so much to see, and the balmy weather that held throughout that week put us in holiday mood. Never could Paris have been more beautiful.

As to our purpose for being in Paris at all, we recognised how important the Exhibition could be to an expanding market, and, in presenting our reports, Colin and I both felt now was the time to make a leap forward into Europe.

On one thing we were all agreed: next year, we would definitely have to be present at the next Paris Yarn Exhibition. It was an occasion to look forward to with keen anticipation.

CHAPTER 13

When we were, that occasion, in Paris, I was content to be anticipating the following year. All that has now changed. I can no longer think beyond the next few days. Suddenly my aims have become very short-term.

Funny how things turn out. When I look back, I suppose the signs were there, if only I'd taken the trouble to take note of them – signs that the body was rebelling against the routine enforced upon it. Stress, some people would say, is the modern killer. Maybe it was just the body wearing itself out on the treadmill of life.

Whatever the cause, the heart refused to bear the brunt any longer. Surgery was the answer, if I was to continue on the treadmill at all. Even then, the signs were not encouraging, and, in the quietness of the night, as I lay sleepless in my hospital bed, my mind seemed to close in upon itself, become totally preoccupied with the uncertainty of the future, and fill me with foreboding.

In the darkness, I learned that there is something about the fear of dying that sharpens the perception of one's existence, and, in this respect, my future was no different from the countless numbers who have faced the same stark reality.

Those 'volunteers', the Pals, of the First World War, for example; many of them came from the mills of our district, they would have known what it was like, as they waited for the signal to go 'over the top'. I could imagine their fear much better now, and could understand a little of what they must have felt – a mixture of bravado, sheer terror, and a passive acceptance that their duty demanded their sacrifice. No matter how brave a face you put on it, death's death, and there's not much fun in that.

Gloomy, morbid thoughts, such as these, ran crazily through my mind, and drove away any thought of sleep.

My plight, though, was nothing so noble as the young men who fought and died in the mud. Mine was far more self-centred; just the hope of clinging on to life for a while longer, to see our children prosper, and, maybe, to see that John, now coming into manhood, was cared for and happy.

If that was to be the case, then I would know in the next few days.

CHAPTER 14

The year is 1987. It is April 23rd, it is morning, and a hazy sun bathes my hospital room in warmth. A gentle spring breeze wafts through an open window to the side of my bed; it feels cool and refreshing.

My day has come – too soon! Why does everything appear normal? Why are people – doctors, nurses, orderlies – not scurrying round the hospital, preparing themselves for the big event, the Match of the Day, the Big Fight? The Final Round?

All's quiet around me; it doesn't seem right. I am allowed a light breakfast, and a nurse brightly ministers to me. Though I have slept only fitfully, I am wide awake now.

I'm told my operation is programmed for noon. Good! Let's get on with it! That's my feeling at the moment. Each time a thought of what's to come flits through my mind, I feel a wave of panic rising within me, then it subsides again, as I console myself with more positive thoughts; if the operation's got to be done, then the surgeons know what they're doing, and I'll be all the better for it. It's like having toothache; if it's a bad tooth, I say to myself, it's got to come out. Well, whatever it is that's preventing my heart from doing its job, it's got to be put right. So stop whingeing.

I realise again how self-absorbed my thoughts have become.

Just as I'm beginning to make more mountains, the door opposite my bed opens, and the welcome, smiling face of Philippa appears. It's good to see her; she looks relaxed, and happy to see me. If she's worried about the day's events, I can't see it in her eyes. I feel reassured again.

Her hands are cool as she sits on the bed beside me. We talk. We talk about things we've done together, experiences we've shared, people we've known. Our reminiscences bring us close together, such as the days when we were courting, and Philippa used to meet me four nights a week when I'd finished night school, and we used to ride home on the bus. Then we talk of our wonderful years in Scotland, the good friends we made, and Jim at the mill. And, of course, we talk of John, our Down's syndrome son, who had made our lives complete. It seems as though we are trying to cram in as many memories as we can in the time left to us – 'just in case' is understood, but neither of us says it.

There is a pause in our chatter, as a nurse busies herself in the room, beginning to get things ready.

Outside, it is a beautiful day. The sun is now high in an almost cloudless sky. I wish I am out of here. The nurse leaves, and we are alone again. For a moment, there is silence.

"Eileen's been to see me about the flowers for the church," says Philippa. Fortunately, I know she is referring to Joanne's wedding, due to take place in the next few weeks. I can't help wondering if I'll be there. That worries me a lot.

"She's good, is Eileen. She'll do a super job for us, I know she will."

"I shall want you to come and help choose my outfit," says Philippa. "It's not something I want to do on my own. I think its got to be a joint decision, don't you?"

"Fine," I say. It's strange how, in the scheme of things, trivial matters assume an importance out of all proportion to their true value.

Things begin happening, and, in moments, I'm on my way.

I realise, too, as she walks alongside the trolley taking me to the operating theatre, that I couldn't have got through the past few weeks without her.

Faint recollections of noisy, bleeping machines, muffled voices, figures dressed in green, water running, bright lights all around me. Then, nothing.

I was floating in a cascade of dreams, brightly-coloured, shimmering, constantly changing, a kaleidoscope of shapes and figures and unreal faces. Then pain, a sharp, stabbing pain, somewhere inside me, I wasn't sure where it hurt me.

"There!" said a distant voice, that sounded like Philippa's. "That's the last of the tubes..."

I struggle to escape the world of dreams, and force myself back into the real world.

Somewhere in that half world between consciousness and unconsciousness, I become aware of more voices, and movement around me.

I open my eyes at last. Warm spring sunshine dazzles me for a
moment. My eyes struggle to come into focus. I turn away from the
brightness, and there is Philippa, her eyes moist with tears. I think I
smile, and her eyes light up.

"It's about time you woke up!" she says, in mock indignation.
"Where've you been for the past three days?"

"Three days?"

"Three days!"

The strained look on Philippa's face tells it all; I can see she's
lived through every second of it. For the first time in weeks, she lets
go for a moment, and tears stream down her cheeks. The feeling of
relief overwhelms us. After a while, she dries her eyes, and she
sniffles quietly.

"Now, as I was saying, about the colour of my outfit for the
wedding..."

I can afford to smile. I know now for certain I'll be at our
Joanne's wedding.

Bruised, battered and bloody, I lie now in my hospital bed.

"Thank God I'm still here," I say to myself. Philippa's red eyes
meet mine. I think we've both just added a new dimension to being
put 'through t'mill'. It's nice to have come through it all, though – so
far.